OUNTERING *the*

ONSPIRACY

to DESTROY

LACK

OYS

Series

Jawanza Kunjufu

Chicago, Illinois

TABLE OF CONTENTS

Foreword

Among the animal and bird kingdoms there are certain species classified as "endangered" by the Department of the Interior. This label has been assigned to these species because they are becoming scarce under adverse environmental conditions and the insatiable greed of man to hunt them for so-called sporting pleasures. Indeed, these species would soon become extinct if it were not for certain laws and protective measures to ensure their survival. However, "endangered species" are not limited to the animal and bird kingdoms. In America, and other nations for that matter, many humans fall under this same category. But this should not come as a revelation. Human life has always been expendable in a world that is bent on violence and war, and which ignores the social and physical needs of many of its inhabitants. And there is no better example of this human neglect than in the case of Black children, or African and African American children.

Jawanza Kunjufu elaborates on this travesty to describe how Europeans, specifically European Americans, have conspired to destroy African Americans by damaging the lives of African American boys. Brother Jawanza chooses to concentrate on the destruction of African American boys because he feels that the African American male poses the greatest threat to White supremacy. During childhood, the system of American racism and oppression begins to cripple African Americans; when they reach adulthood, they are socially, physically and politically impotent. Although the reader may question his emphasis on African American boys over African American girls, one cannot easily dismiss the fact that European Americans have done nearly everything imaginable to malign and subjugate African American males. In his commentary, Brother Jawanza describes how African American boys are systematically programmed for failure so that when they become adults they pose little danger to the status quo. By their control of key social institutions, European Americans have denied the African American boy the fruits of his heritage, culture and "rights of passage." As a result, the African American boy becomes the bearer of social maladies which he carries with him into adulthood. This "early seasoning" is described by Sekou Toure, president of Guinea, as the "science of dehumanization" which signals the first stage of the conspiracy.

Brother Jawanza cites the public school as being the most flagrant institution which contributes to the destruction of African American boys. This destruction can be clearly observed during the fourth grade when many African American boys begin to exhibit signs of intellectual retrogression. Unfortunately, most never recover, and as a result, a disproportionate number of African American students find themselves ill-prepared to survive in a racist educational system. However, Brother Jawanza feels that a strong school principal, an aroused and concerned community, and positive role models can do much to change this disparaging situation. He suggests that more African American male teachers be assigned to the primary grades because it is during the formative years that children shape their values and begin to identify with role models. But the public school ignores this fact and does little to encourage males to teach in the primary grades.

The author is also highly critical of the "macho syndrome" which permeates the society. Many African American men seem to be mesmerized by this chauvinistic quality. In their effort to compensate for certain weaknesses, they become strong advocates of the "macho syndrome," displaying it like a badge of honor. African American boys must be taught that masculinity is not measured by the size of one's biceps or sexual powers, but is a quality that is characterized by being affectionate, sincere and responsible.

Brother Jawanza also stresses the importance of a strong family unit as being the foundation for the positive development of African American children. Despite its weaknesses, the Black family unit should not be perceived as being an anemic institution. Contrary to what we are led to believe, there are strengths in this unit that need to be considered in programming for African American children.

Although the picture which Brother Jawanza depicts is not a glamorous one, it is not etched in stone. The author makes it unmistakably clear that something can be done to correct the dehumanization of African American children. He understands, and quite correctly, that all too often the African American community accepts its problems as being insurmountable. The system of racism and oppression is designed to foster this type of passive resignation. However, Brother Jawanza does not leave the reader with a sense of hopelessness. He offers many examples of what can be done to ensure that African American boys grow up to be strong, committed and responsible African American men. But he does warn us that unless we seriously respond to the true needs of African boys, the future of African Americans is indeed bleak and destined to follow the path of other endangered species.

Brother Jawanza should be commended for this insightful work. As a long-time advocate for African American children, he has synthesized these two disciplines and provided us with a commentary that should be read by everyone who is concerned about African American children - the seeds of our destiny and ultimate liberation.

Useni Eugene Perkins

Introduction

I wrote the first volume of Countering the Conspiracy to Destroy Black Boys in 1982. The Lord inspired me to write it after witnessing a disproportionate number of African American males in special education, suspension, and scores declining after fourth grade. Every four years the Lord has blessed me to write another volume. I released volume II in 1986, Volume III in 1990, and Volume IV in 1994. The combined volumes have over a million copies in print.

This hardback, revised, updated, and expanded version is designed for my new readers who hadn't read the earlier volumes. It is also being provided for my loyal enduring readers who either prefer all four volumes together in a hardback edition or who have loaned one or more of the volumes and for some strange reason they were never returned!

I have often been asked why I concentrate more on boys than men. I have believed over the past two decades that the problems African American men are experiencing did not begin when they were incarcerated at 21 years of age. I don't believe the problems men have keeping their word, showing up for work on time and raising their children began in adulthood.

I believe in prevention. Therefore, I feel it is easier to develop a boy into a man which is a one-step process than it is removing bad habits from men and providing them with an Africentric, Maatian view of the world, which is a two-step process. I also believe the most effective way to destroy the African American family is to destroy the African American man, which places a greater burden on the African American woman to raise her children, specifically her male children in a racist, patriarchal and capitalistic society.

I am thankful that as a boy growing up I had the best father a son could have. I was also blessed to have excellent male teachers and a track coach who taught me kujichagulia (self-determination). I was also exposed to some of the greatest speakers and writers in my collegiate experience. For the above reasons, I disagree with Shelby Steele and Clarence Thomas who resent being asked to volunteer and become mentors to African American males. I believe to whom much is given, much is required. Consequently, we need to volunteer our time, talents and monies to "the least of these."

Lastly, over the course of these four volumes, I have seen my two sons grow into adulthood. I thank God they are still alive and my prayer remains they will love the Lord, strive for excellence and work for their race.

$\mathcal{C}$HAPTER $\mathcal{O}$NE

The Conspiracy to Destroy Black Boys

Genocide (jen' ə sid')n. The deliberate and systematic destruction of a racial, political or cultural group.

To use the word *conspiracy* to describe certain aspects of our society is a strong indictment against the social fabric of this country. I have been challenged hundreds of times in debates and by the media with the use of this word *conspiracy*. Many of the challengers want me to document who were the plotters of this conspiracy, where was the meeting and when did it take place? I smile and listen to their barrage and remain confident in knowing as Neely Fuller stated, "until you understand White supremacy, everything else will confuse you." I then begin to ask them several questions:

1) Can you explain how less than 10 percent of the world's population which is White own over 70 percent of the world's wealth?
2) Can you explain how every United States president has been a White male?
3) Is there a relationship between Africans being labeled three-fifths of a person and their median income being that same fraction in comparison to Whites?
4) Why did some Whites feel the need to physically castrate African American males?
5) Was it an accident that all the men that constituted the "Tuskegee Experiment" were African American and they possessed syphilis and went untreated by the U.S. Center for Disease Control for 40 years?
6) Is it ironic that only two White persons have ever received the death penalty for killing an African American?
7) Are the video tapes of racial discrimination as shown on national television in housing, banking, employment and shopping a figment of our imagination?

8) Is it an accident that African American males comprise six percent of the U.S. population, but represent 35 percent of the special education children and 50 percent of the inmates?

Could the above be happenstance, irony, luck or a conspiracy?

9) Is it an accident that on average a white male with a high-school diploma earns more than anyone else in America on average with a college degree?

10) Is it luck that one percent of the U.S. population owns 48 percent of the wealth and greater than 99 percent of them are White?

11) Was it ironic that the F.B.I. used their program "Cointelpro" to infiltrate African American organizations with their stated objectives: to create internal conflict and prevent a messianic leader?

There is a broad array of people ranging from historians, politicians, academicians and writers who have provided the "theoretical" justification for White supremacy.

Cecil Rhodes, in his article "Confessions of Faith," provides the historical blueprint:

> I contend that we are the finest race in the world and that the more of the world we inhabit the better it is for the human race. Just fancy those parts that are at present inhabited by the most despicable specimens of human beings. What an alteration there would be if they were brought under Anglo-Saxon influence. Look again at the extra employment a new country added to our dominion gives. Why should we not form a secret society with but one object, the furtherance of the British Empire and the bringing of the whole uncivilized world under British rule? Poverty is better under our flag than wealth under a foreign one. Africa is still lying ready for us, it is our duty to seize every opportunity to acquire more territory and we should keep this one idea steadily before our eyes that more territory simply means more of the Anglo-Saxon race, more of the best of the most human, most honorable race this world possesses.[1]

Arnold Toynbe (historian) states,

> When we classify mankind by color, the only one of the primary races . . . which has not made a creative contribution to civilization is the Black race.

Thomas Jefferson wrote,

> I advanced it, that the Blacks are inferior to the Whites in the endowments of both body and mind.

Abraham Lincoln wrote,

> There is a physical difference between the White and the Black race. There must be the position of superior and inferior, and I as much as any man am in favor of having the superior position assigned to the White race.[2]

Holly Sklar, in the book *Trilateralism*, notes:

> Very few women have been admitted into elite planning circles; there are virtually no women in the inner circles. Women were not admitted to the Council on Foreign Relations until 1970. No women serve as chief executive officers and only a handful have reached high positions in the corporations related to the Trilateral Commission.[3]

Sidney Wilhelm comments in *Who Needs the Negro*,

> The ultimate destiny of the Afro-American is likely to be extermination, not assimilation. His situation is less like that of the European immigrant than like that of the American Indian. Black militants have not fully understood the economic basis of what they perceive, but in prophesying genocide they have accurately grasped the end to which logic of automation leads.[4]

Ralph Epperson in *The New World Order* writes,

> We can no longer afford freedom, and so it must be replaced with control over his conduct and his culture. Two centuries ago our forefathers brought forth a new nation; now we must joint with others to bring forth a new world order.[5]

The legacy of White supremacy arguments continues with Charles Murray and Richard Herrnstein in the *Bell Curve*, who believe that IQ is substantially heritable somewhere between 40 and 80 percent, meaning that much of the observed variation in IQ is genetic.

I wonder how the authors scientifically determined the range 40-80 percent? Second, that is a broad range for a scientific argument. Lastly, how did they do what no other scholar has been able to and that is separate the impact of genetics from environment to develop their conclusions?

I believe five of the best African American scholars to explain the origins and motivations of White supremacy are:

Cheikh Anta Diop - Civilization or Barbarism
Bobby Wright   - Psychopathic Racial Personality
Marimba Ani   - Yurugu
Neely Fuller Jr.   - United Independent Compensatory
                             Code/System/Concept
Frances C. Welsing - Isis Papers

Welsing states,

> Racism is viewed as a global behavior power system with a constant and specific set of power relationships. Racism evolved with the singular goal of white supremacy or white power domination by the global white minority over the vast non-white global majority. This "colored global collective" has been forced into the position of relative powerlessness compared to the "global white collective" establishing the power equation of white over non-white (W/N-W). Racism, whether consciously or unconsciously evolved as a survival necessity for the tiny global white minority, due to their genetic recessive status as albino variants (mutants) in a world of skin-color genetically dominant black, brown, red and yellow peoples. Indeed had the global white minority not evolved this specific system of power relationships (whites over non-whites) wherein whites control all of the behavior activity of non-whites in all areas of people activity (economics, education, entertainment, labor, law, politics, religion,

sex and war) as a survival mechanism, in the presence of the genetically dominant colored world majority, the mutant albino genetic-recessive minority would find itself genetically annihilated. That is there would be no "white" people except for the new mutations to albinism produced by skin-melaninated or colored peoples. Thus, to prevent the genetic annihilation of skin whiteness, a behavior power system was evolve—the power system of racism or white supremacy domination.[6]

Men initiate the act of reproduction. Therefore, if a population is fearful of its genetic annihilation, it has to focus only on the men of the potentially annihilating population. When you consider an African man, African woman, European man, and European woman, there are four possible heterosexual combinations, but only one will produce a child with genetic makeup similar to Europeans:

African man	— African woman	= dominant genes
African man	— European woman	= dominant genes
European man	— African woman	= dominant genes
European man	— European woman	= recessive genes

We must now expand our description of racism to include imperialism and White male supremacy.

I smile when asked to prove that White male supremacy exists because, as Bobby Wright in the *Psychopathic Racial Personality* reminds us, a racist has no conscience or memory and is in a classic state of denial. Therefore, I spend no time trying to trigger a racist's consciousness. Second, in any conspiracy there would be two major players - active and passive. The active conspirators have been described above, some are overt racists and others are covert and participate through institutions. These are the "liberals" I meet on talk shows who say, "I didn't take your people from Africa. I'm struggling in America just like you. Can't we all just get along?"

Now, let's look at a more subtle form of the conspiracy, institutional racism.

Two college graduates, with identical grade-point averages and majors, apply for the same position with an employer. The African American graduate is interviewed first and is told by the European employer either that the position has been filled or that he is not appropriate for the position. Upon leaving the employer's office, he mentions to his European friend to leave, based on the information he received. The other graduate decides, just for the experience, he would like to be interviewed, and secures the position. The European graduate did not make the final decision, nor did he deny the benefit his racial position affords him. Taking advantage of a situation, whether in employment, housing or other opportunities, is playing a passive role in the conspiracy and perpetuates institutional racism.

The passive conspirators are African Americans who participate via their miseducation, self-hatred and apathy. This group consists of African American males who do not raise their children. It also includes African American women who have double standards for their children. They have lower expectations for their sons than their daughters. This group includes African American educators who also have lowered their expectations for African American children, specifically the male child. It also includes those that sell drugs and commit murders.

I am not confident that we can convert a racist who is xenophobic to a secure loving person who is xenophillic. I expect nothing less from African Americans than for them to disavow from consciously or unconsciously participating in their own genocide and to actively become involved in the liberation of their own people.

Chapter Two

Infancy - Nine Years

Over the years I have grown tired of hearing about the adult African American shortage. Oftentimes the books, conferences, radio and television specials border on sensationalism. The topic has become good business. We seem to look at this issue only from a macro perspective, forgetting that each of the 17 to 20 million African American males should be viewed individually. In this way we can determine what is needed to develop boys into responsible African American men. We have a small shortage at birth, but all newborn African American girls born today statistically should have an ample number of men to choose from in the future.

It is remarkable how the Lord works in the production of life. The chances of a sperm fertilizing an egg and developing through the entire birth cycle are one in a million. Unfortunately, in the African American community, the chances of a successful birth are even more remote due to the lack of pre— and post-natal care. The normal birth weight is 5.5 lbs, and 13 percent of African American children are underweight, in contrast to six percent for Whites. The infant mortality rate for African American children is 18 deaths per 1,000 live births in comparison to 9 per 1,000 Whites. Black boys survive less than girls: 1,965 deaths per 100,000 live births versus girls' 1,603 per 100,000.[1]

The African American community resembles an underdeveloped country in relation to the quality of care provided for expectant mothers and infants. In most large urban areas, one-tenth of African American babies are addicted to drugs. Have you ever seen an adult withdrawn from heroin or cocaine? The experience does not even compare to the trauma experienced by the infant whose first nine months were dependent on its substance. Seventy percent of all African American children

7

are born out of wedlock. Female African American teenagers lead the industrialized world in teen pregnancy, followed by Arab and European Americans. I often ask the Lord if He would consider reversing the responsibility and allowing the males to become pregnant. I was pleased to see Cosby allocate a show to this phenomenon. I honestly believe that the teen pregnancy epidemic would subside in our community if the brothers got pregnant, as depicted below.

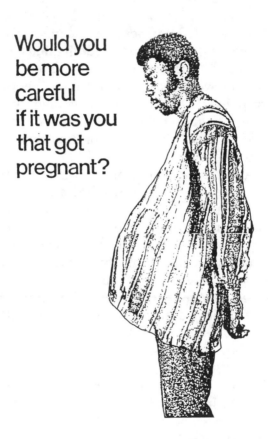

Would you be more careful if it was you that got pregnant?

We would have birth control all over the town, like Europe, if this were to happen. We need more programs like Project Alpha and Teen Fathers that stress both male and female responsibility.

Frances Welsing suggests that to correct this problem in our race and to restore our people to their original greatness, we should delay marriage until the age of 28. By then maturation should have taken place, along with the development of self-esteem. A couple should then wait until age 30 before having children; this would allow the couple to become better acquainted and discuss their views on child rearing. There are few things worse than to marry someone with different views on child rearing. The couple should only have two children, bearing them four years apart; each child would then receive an adequate amount of individual nurturance, or "lap time," before the next child is born. Ironically, those with the *least* to give - time, money, nurturance, and direction - have the *most* children, and those with the *most* to give have the *fewest*. The future of our race depends on only bringing into the world children that are loved, nurtured and given a sense of direction. Nation building is not built on *quantity* but *quality*.

In contrast to Frances Welsing's theory of 28, 30, 2 and 4, in many of our communities, the rule of thumb has become 0, 13, 5 or more children every nine months. (Many couples are not married, mothers give birth at age 13, and have five children every nine months.) We are not going to develop our race with that kind of lifestyle. From this point on, we will hone in on the specific problems and peculiarities that are affecting African American males. Many people are aware of the large disparity between African American males and females as it relates to incarceration, homicide, suicide, alcoholism and other ills. Most people are not aware that Black boys also lead Black girls in infant mortality, as previously mentioned. Consequently, the male shortage begins early (though many people think that the male shortage begins at age 18, 25, or 30). In actuality the male shortage begins at birth when there is a disproportionate number of Black boys that aren't able to survive birth. At the tender ages of two weeks, one month and three months, African American females are already experiencing the Black male shortage.

The future of African Americans is dependent on us developing our boys to be men.

The next period that we want to concentrate on is the pre-school years, the period between six months and four to five years of age. This is a very important period. Many doctors and psychologists have pointed out that the brain's growth and development is greatest between infancy and three years of age, with the next-greatest period being between three and six years of age. It becomes crucial that the African American community develop our children, especially our boys, during this critical period of brain development and cognitive growth. This area of child development is paramount in reinforcing fine motor and language development.

Instead, we have a frightening situation in which many of our children, having been born addicted to drugs, are experiencing the effects of detoxification. In addition, many children live in homes where fine and gross motor and language development are not encouraged. These are the reasons why many people advocate Home Start, Head Start and other programs to develop these skills even before the child enters kindergarten. This reinforces the notion of professionals who say that the most important periods are between infancy and three, followed by three to five, in child development. These are the times when parents should be cradling their children close to them; toys should be bought for their ability to stimulate cognitive and motor development as well as for fun. For example, cradle gyms can be attached to the cradle to maximize development. It is remarkable how energetic and intelligent African American children are, especially if they are placed in environments with the proper nurturance, nutrition and guidance that all children should receive.

There are numerous studies that have been done around the world contrasting and comparing what children are able to do at certain stages. One such study done by several doctors compared African and European American children and their ability to recognize and respond to stimuli.

1. With body drawn up into a sitting position, able to prevent the head from falling backwards - African, nine hours; European, six weeks.
2. With head held firmly, able to look at face of the examiner - African, two days; European, eight weeks.

3. Able to support body in a sitting position and watch reflection in the mirror - African, seven weeks; European, 20 weeks.
4. Able to hold body upright - African, five months; European, nine months.
5. Able to take the round block out of its hold in the formboard - African, five months; European, 11 months.
6. Can stand against the mirror - African, five months; European, nine months.
7. Can walk to the Gesell box to look inside - African, seven months; European, 15 months.
8. Can climb steps alone - African, 11 months; European, 15 months.[2]

These studies are very significant because if we really want to measure natural and raw intelligence, this would be the best time to do it, between infancy and three years of age. From that point on, we're really measuring what children have been exposed to, not intelligence. It becomes discouraging that our children, at a very young age, have demonstrated a tremendous amount of intelligence, only to place last on high school culture tests. The above indicators of innate intelligence show that in the first three years, African American children are exceptional. Psychologists and educators have always recommended that parents talk, read and play games with their children. This will help in their growth and development.

In dissecting the first stage of growth and development in Black males from infancy to nine years of age, there are two major components that I want to analyze. One is the dichotomy between fine motor and gross motor development, and the second is the issue of hyperactivity.

Comparing males and females in fine motor and gross motor development, the female body on the average is 23 percent muscle; the male body is 40 percent muscle.[3] Right or wrong, schools value fine motor development more so than gross motor development.

How well children can hold a pencil, a crayon, or a pair of scissors (fine motor) is valued more than their ability to hold a ball, play with a truck, grab an object and wrestle with one another (gross motor). "Boys will be boys," families like to say.

Given two young children at home, the daughter will be coloring and the son will be playing with his truck, car or basketball. This is a very complicated point: Are we saying that we want to take gross motor objects away from Black boys and force them at the tender ages of two and three to sit still with crayons, pencils, and scissors? Or are we saying that we should take the pencils and pens and scissors away from girls and give them trucks, balls and large motor objects to manipulate? Or are we suggesting that schools find other ways to measure learning besides a left brain, analytical, fine motor approach? Schools must realize that intelligence can be measured in other ways *besides a left brain abstract exam.* All these factors need to be considered, but ultimately what we are trying to do is develop Black boys into men.

The first step in achieving this is not to compare boys to girls and assume that boys are deficient. Diane McGuinness has written an excellent book on the subject called *When Children Don't Learn.* Many people have often wondered, Are boys and girls different? While we have some general feelings and differences, how do we allow for those differences in preschool programs, kindergarten, primary, intermediate and upper grades? It becomes a matter of concern when 75 percent of children in remedial reading are male.[4] This applies to both Black and White males.

Somehow we have the general sentiment that boys and girls are different; yet we have not allowed for those differences in the home and in the classroom so that boys and girls can develop according to their own unique abilities. If we define growth and development from a female perspective (i.e., how long you can sit still, or how well you can hold a pencil, crayon, or pair of scissors), then we may be defining success in a way that will be detrimental to male growth and development. Diane McGiunness points out in her book that there is a relationship between reading and hearing. Studies have confirmed that in order to read, you have to be able to hear the syllables. Females' hearing abilities are greater than males.

> The response of the human ear at auditory threshold has maximum sensitivity of about 1,000 cycles per second (cps). This is approximately "high C" on the

We must develop boys' fine motor skills in preschool.

musical scale. Hearing becomes less and less efficient both above and below this frequency, until all sounds become completely inaudible below 20 cps and above 20,000 cps, which is the limit of human hearing. When we get older or expose our ears to very loud sounds, such as factory noise or rock music, the upper range of hearing deteriorates.

When the sexes are compared, females show a greater sensitivity at threshold for sounds above 3,000 cps, and their sensitivity relative to males improves at higher frequencies. The sex differences become more pronounced with age, and women suffer much less hearing loss than men. Females were found to have greater sensitivity above 3,000 cps. I have found very similar results on a population of fifty college students. These results help us to understand part of the females' advantage in the development of language, because high-frequency sensitivity is particularly important in the accurate perception of certain speech sounds, especially the consonants c, s, t, x and z.

In tests of comfortable loudness the sex differences are perhaps the greatest. I asked fifty British college students to increase the volume of sound until it became "just too loud." The women set considerably lower levels of volume than the men across a broad range of frequencies. The difference between the sexes was a constant 7 to 8 decibels across the entire frequency range (see figure 2.1).

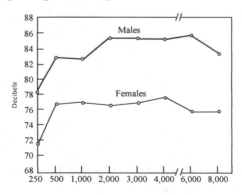

Diane McGuinness, *When Children Don't Learn* p. 78[5]

15

Later in the chapter, as we move into the primary grade period between kindergarten and third grade, we will discuss this research in more detail and its implications for reading abilities. For now we are looking at the period between six months and three to four years of age. We are looking at the fine and the gross motor skills and language development of our children as they relate to the home.

It becomes imperative that schools acknowledge that males and females mature at different rates. Research indicates that girls mature about two years ahead of boys. Unless schools are willing to make some adjustments in evaluating and labeling children, then the only alternative is for parents to accept female expectations for their male children. Parents can try to accelerate their sons' growth and development by greater utilization of fine motor objects and strengthening their hearing abilities by reading to them and reducing loud music, especially loud rap music, which impairs hearing of young Black boys.

Two schools of thought emerged to try and explain the developmental differences between boys and girls. Alfred Binet, a psychologist, developed a test that, unfortunately, ended up being used to classify children; even he acknowledged that the test should have been used as an indicator. However, many educators advocate classifying children. Some people feel comfortable when they can put children into categories. This comes out of a left-brain school of thought, where there is a need to place people and objects into divisions. This tendency is prevalent in the music industry. When people try to make Nancy Wilson and Wynton Marsalis choose what category of music they sing and play, they consistently say, "I'm a singer, or I'm a musician. I'll perform while you classify." The same approach takes place in our schools.

Maria Montessori, a medical doctor, based her approach on the fact that children develop at different rates (males vs. females, Blacks vs. Whites), and that there's nothing wrong with children developing or learning at different rates or with different styles. We should design homes and classrooms to allow for those differences and to encourage children to expose themselves in ways that are comfortable. Unfortunately, the Montessori approach is least used in our

16

schools; classification dominates. As a result, a high number of male children are labeled hyperactive and dyslexic; then they are placed in remedial reading classes, and ultimately, special education.

The second area that I want to look at is hyperactivity. The energy level of African American children is referred to by some psychologists as "verve." The word "hyperactive" is a value judgment. The word is based on an assumption that we have an understanding and knowledge of what normal activity represents. It may be that African American children, and specifically African American male children, are not hyperactive. It may be that the stimuli around them are simply not challenging enough. They choose to become involved with other activities that they find to be of greater interest.

There was a study done by Yale University that looked at two very popular television shows, *Mr. Rogers* and *Sesame Street.* Mr. Rogers is a very slow moving show. Sesame Street is more action oriented; the images change more frequently. Yale University found that African American children responded better to *Sesame Street* and European children responded better to *Mr. Rogers.*[6] Unfortunately, the average classroom moves at a pace similar to the *Mr. Rogers* show. Therefore, it may not be that African American children, and specifically African American male children, are hyperactive. It may be that the methodology is simply too slow. Interesting enough, boys of all races do not seem to be hyperactive when they play video games or when they are involved in other activities that capture their interest.

Shown in *Figures* 2.2 and 2.3 are the results of a study measuring children's level of interest in various activities, which reinforces the conclusion that hyperactivity may not be the issue. What children are involved with will determine their interest level. We may need to look at the stimuli we provide for children rather than label them hyperactive when they do not respond as we deem appropriate.

Figure 2.2 illustrates the scores for the average duration in minutes for each of these categories. Perseverance, for example, was calculated as the longest time a child spent on any one activity during the period of observation. The average time for the girls was twelve minutes, for the boys, eight minutes.

Girls spent twice as much time in play organized by the teacher (usually, but not always, a female), whereas males spent twice as much time in unsupervised play constructing things or watching other children.

Figure 2.3 illustrates the frequency of occurrence of certain behaviors. Boys are found to carry out four and one-half different activities in twenty minutes, girls only two and one-half.

Figure 2.2

HYPERACTIVITY: A Diagnosis in Search of a Patient

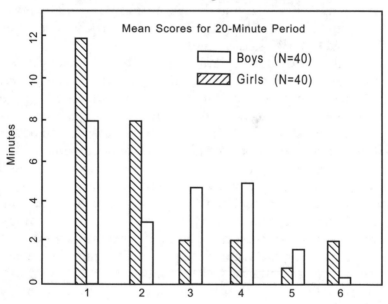

1-Longest Time Spent on One Activity
2-Time Spent in Teacher-Organized Activity
3-Time Spent in Construction-Toy Play
4-Time Spent Watching Others
5-Longest Time Watching Others
6-Time Spent Painting Alone

Diane McGuinnes, *When Children Don't Learn*[7]

Particularly interesting is the number of interruptions of ongoing play. Boys interrupted what they were doing three times more frequently than girls. Behaviors in categories 7 to 9, which were intended to tap destructive and aggressive behaviors, occurred extremely infrequently. None of our observers ever saw any serious misbehavior, and no child at this excellent preschool was considered deviant, hyperactive or difficult to control. Therefore, a sex difference of the magnitude we discovered is all the more remarkable and illustrates that when children are left to their own devices, "boys time their actions differently than girls."

Figure 2.3

HYPERACTIVITY: Unraveling the Evidence

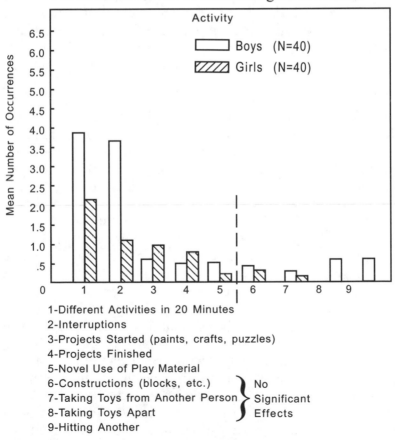

1-Different Activities in 20 Minutes
2-Interruptions
3-Projects Started (paints, crafts, puzzles)
4-Projects Finished
5-Novel Use of Play Material
6-Constructions (blocks, etc.) ⎫
7-Taking Toys from Another Person ⎬ No Significant Effects
8-Taking Toys Apart ⎪
9-Hitting Another ⎭

Diane McGuinnes, *When Children Don't Learn*

In a classroom setting, the routine and structure favors the timing patterns of girls far more than that of boys. Imposing these unnatural temporal constraints on young boys can disrupt their normal rhythms, producing frustration and tension.

The African American home is filled with a great number of stimuli. Many psychologists and social workers who have not lived or been trained in the African American experience label the African American home as chaotic. A home that has five or more children, two or three radios playing at the same time on different stations, extended-family members entering and exiting the home, is for many educators, psychologists and social workers, quite overwhelming. Children that come out of these kinds of homes have developed an ability to do more than one task at the same time. They are more people - than object-oriented and prefer interacting with children rather than objects. A child being raised in a home with only one sibling or none, performing only one task at a time and doing home-work only when it's quiet is geared more toward the American classroom. Again, we are faced with a dilemma.

Schools need to understand that children with higher energy levels are not hyperactive; they simply have a higher verve. The level of intelligence demonstrated by African children during infancy confirms that innate talent exists, and schools should be charged with creating an environment that maximizes cognition with classifications. Many of us are doing all that we can to provide in-service training to teachers to help them better understand the relationship between culture and learning styles, but people and institutions move very slowly. So we have to place pressure on African American homes to reduce the stimuli in order to match the American classroom. I stated earlier that we may need to reduce the trucks, basketballs and gross motor objects that are given to our boys and increase the number of fine motor tools boys need to be involved with in preparation for kindergarten and the primary grades.

We also recommend that African American homes reduce the music. Many teachers have indicated that there is simply no quiet time at home, and their classroom is not going to teach reading with *Jay Z, Nas, Little Kim,* and *50 Cent* playing in the background. From three o'clock to nine o'clock there is a greater degree of noise in many of our homes. It becomes imperative, if we are going to reduce the number of African American children, and specifically - African American male children, from being hyperactive, then parents and teachers must compromise. Parents need to institute quiet time where children are expected to sit still for a few minutes. As they become older, teachers have greater expectations on the number of minutes children can sit still. Playing games such as "Concentration" and "Simon Says" enhances listening skills and following directions which, teachers say, are most problematic in African American boys. Parents can cultivate their male child's development by reading and discussing ideas together. This interaction will give you an opportunity to evaluate your child's development personally.

We must also develop our children's social skills. They must be taught manners and respect for authority. When children enter preschool, kindergarten and primary grades, teachers are very concerned about children's social skills. They observe how well children interact with one another, and whether they are respectful and cooperative with each other.

Many teachers feel that African American boys are very aggressive. There is an African proverb that says, "It takes a *whole* village to raise *a* child," not a single parent or two parents - a village. Unfortunately, many African American parents are telling their children, "You don't have to respect anybody but me." As a result, children at a young age are telling their teachers, neighbors, and other adults, "You're not my mama, you can't tell me what to do." One of the major strengths of Asian children, besides being obedient, exhibiting discipline and valuing education, is their respect for authority, which means respect for their elders. African American boys may have the greatest problem in respecting authority figures. The aggression being expressed in the classroom, to their own detriment, contributes heavily to being placed in special education classes.

We as parents have to ask ourselves, "Have we given our boys the resources necessary to have a successful academic and social experience?" We have to ask ourselves as educators, "Are we going to provide a fair opportunity for boys in the classroom without comparing them to girls, European American and Asian American children? Have we provided the experience

21

and the environment that will allow boys to grow to their fullest potential?"

Now we face the next hurdle, kindergarten. Children, specifically African American male children, are failing. It has now reached an epidemic level, where you can now fail kindergarteners. This was unheard of ten, fifteen or twenty years ago. The self-esteem of a child failing kindergarten is greatly affected. From this point on in their educational career, they will be one year behind everyone else. They will have to explain to the other children every year why their age and grade do not correspond.

The National Association of Educating Young Children (NAEYC) has gone on record in trying to persuade educators to refrain from comparing children. Some children receive their first formal educational experience as early as six months old, others in kindergarten. Kindergarten teachers cannot determine what children are bringing to them. Teachers should take children as they are and develop them with the curriculum that was designed at the kindergarten level.

Is it fair to a child who was not taught his/her numbers, alphabets and colors before the first day of kindergarten to be placed in the slowest group and labeled "at risk?" Kindergarten used to be the grade where children were introduced to colors, alphabets, numbers, the spelling of their names, social skills and fine motor skills. Due to the wide disparity in income levels and other socioeconomic factors, many parents have prepared their children before kindergarten with some of these skills. Rather than accepting this, educators negatively evaluate children that have not been exposed to these learning skills, therefore tracking unfortunately begins at the kindergarten level.

Many parents and community people in large urban areas ponder the reasons for the high dropout rate of 50 percent and upward. Children can be in the ninth grade and read on a third through fifth grade level. (A wide disparity among students exists in the same classroom.) The difference begins before children enter into the formal kindergarten experience. I'm appealing to African American parents to expose their children to the kinds of experiences that they are going to be expected to master in kindergarten. It is also an opportunity for teachers and educators to again assess whether they're providing an opportunity that is fair to all children. Whatever academic achievement levels existed between one child and another before kindergarten *widens* with their educational experience because of tracking. Tracking begins as early as the eighth day of kindergarten. Teachers divide students into ability groups.[8]

First, how much academic information do teachers have on a child on the eighth day of kindergarten? They have very little. They rely on the social worker's interview and the parental registration forms. They also look at how children are dressed, the way they smell, whether they are verbal with adults, whether they speak Black English, whether a father is in the home, whether they're low-income and what their energy level is in the classroom. Children that do not meet the teacher's feminine, middle-class standard are placed in the lowest reading group. The study goes on to point out that the children in the lowest reading group receive the lowest level of expectations. The study which was a longitudinal study, also demonstrates that other children also evaluated as early as the eighth day of kindergarten, were placed in the highest reading group. Both groups remained in the respective group throughout the first and second grade. This initial classification has now become a self-fulfilling prophecy. If this format continues throughout the primary, intermediate and upper grades, we're going to see a large differential which was created by "at risk schools," not "at risk children."

African American children comprise 17 percent of public school children in this nation and 41 percent of children placed in special education. Why the disproportionate number? We believe that any percentage greater than 17 is excessive. To further compound the problem, 85 percent of those African American children are male. We believe that any percentage beyond 50 is also too high and that before we look at the boys, we have to look at educators and the school environment and ask ourselves, "What is it about the environment and our assessment tools that promote the placing of Black boys in special education more than Black girls, and the placing of African American children in special education more than European American children?"

If the ideal student is a female, and is quiet, cooperative and attempts to please the teacher, and in contrast, if boys are aggressive, possess a high energy level and do not always cooperate with teachers, does that dictate that boys of all races deserve to be 90 percent of the children labeled hyperactive, 75 percent of the children placed in remedial reading and 85 percent of the children placed in special education?

The problem is further compounded when many people do not value statistics and acknowledge only personal experiences. If we have a class of thirty students, consisting of fifteen males and fifteen females, and five of the male students are labeled "special ed," we can look at this situation in one of two ways: We can either say the problem is with the five boys and their behavior, because the other ten boys do not have this same problem, or we can say that when you have one-third of your males negatively classified, there needs to be a reassessment of our measurement tools.

We have two boys in our class. The first boy's name is Darryl. He is very quiet, nonathletic, cooperative and fearful of strangers. The other kindergarten student is Richard. He's athletic, very talkative and popular. Darryl, by most teachers' standards, will be a good student. Richard will be viewed with suspicion. If academic intelligence was not valued to the exclusion of social, kinetic, athletic, spatial, and musical intelligence, then Richard would also be intelligent.

Another example: We have four levels of students: low-income, middle-class, White, and Black students. The teacher reads the children a story. The middle-and low-income White students and middle-income African American students regurgitate the story back to the teacher exactly as it was read to them. Rote learning and memorization are taking place. The lower-income Black students jazz it up. They bring in some additional characters, put in a little body movement, make it more interesting, original, convincing and dramatic. If we only value rote learning, three groups receive an A, and the last group fails. If we also value original, dramatic and convincing, then the last group would also receive an A.

Unfortunately, in most American schools the last group would not have received an A because we measure intelligence and academic achievement in very narrow parameters. If African

American children cannot perform within those dimensions then they are labeled in ways that determine their future.

I mentioned earlier in the chapter that there are physical differences between males and females. Whether we look at the development of muscles, hearing abilities or the overall maturation rate of boys and girls, there are differences. The question is, Do we allow for those differences in the classroom? It is obvious from the statistics that we have done a very poor job of acknowledging the differences in males and females and in Africans and Europeans.

The factors that contribute to the disproportionate number of African American males in special education exceed racism. Sexism is a part of it. When 83 percent of your teaching staff is female, 92 percent of your teaching staff is White, and only 1.2 percent of your teaching staff is African American male, there is a very good chance that the group that's least represented (African American males) is going to receive the brunt of the improper or inappropriate labeling that's taking place in our school system. A whole book could be written on the relationship between female teachers and African American male students. In my earlier book, *Critical Issues in Educating African American Youth*, I indicated that the most important factor for the growth and development of children is not the *race* or the *gender* of the teacher but his/her *expectations.* I maintain that position. This does not negate my concern about the relationship between White female teachers and Black male students. This relationship leads to great misunderstandings and a lack of bonding; yet it is a very frequent occurrence, and it's going to increase as the number of African American teachers declines.

Males and females learn in different ways; they mature at different rates. White boys also suffer from this educational system, but because of a world based on White male supremacy, a White boy with a high school diploma will receive more money than a White or Black female or Black male with a college degree. Black boys are not as fortunate to have fathers who may own a corporation. They are not likely to benefit from White male privilege.

To remedy the problem of disproportionate numbers of Black boys in remedial reading, special education and being labeled hyperactive, schools must realize that children learn differently, and parents must establish quiet time, introduce fine motor activities, teach respect for authority figures and improve so-social graces. In addition to the solutions, we will also introduce or develop the notion of an all-Black-male classroom, a class-room consisting of only Black boys being taught by a Black male teacher. This solution would remove the opportunity to compare boys and girls. Boys would not be faced with the pressure of having to act like girls, presently considered the ideal students. Another possibility is to delay boys' entry into kindergarten by one or two years because of the maturation difference. In this way we will not have a five-year-old boy competing with a five-year-old girl. Obviously, these two are not ideal solutions.

However, it is a fact: girls mature about two years ahead of boys, but this could be offset in schools that, when classifying children, would consider gender differences. For example, boys may not be behind in reading if we only compared males to males, rather than comparing male scores to the scores of all students. Males may be two years behind girls in reading but they may not be two years behind each other. In this context, if a girl was two years behind other female students, then that girl would go into remedial reading along with all the boys that were two years behind other male students. This way, we will be comparing apples to apples.

It may not be that boys are poor readers; it may be that boys simply mature and develop reading skills more slowly than girls. Studies also indicate that boys are more spatially and visually developed (which may explain their interest in playing videos), and that boys are more advanced in mathematics, especially higher-older mathematics, including, geometry and trigonom-etry, because they rely more on spatial and visual development.

The primary teacher, kindergarten through third grade, pro-vides a more holistic learning approach than any other group. My interest is for teachers fourth through twelfth grade to also realize that children learn in different ways. It is in the primary division that teachers use fewer ditto sheets in preference of the oral traditions, including pictures, fine arts and artifacts. From the fourth grade on, we use a left-brain, written, analytical approach to teaching children. I wish we had more primary grade teachers teaching in the upper grades who would use a right-brain pedagogy to present a lesson, especially to the African American male child who often prefers learning in other ways. It is in the primary grade that you see children involved in drawing, music, drama and other models of learning.

The male shortage that we hear so much about is smaller at infancy. At this level we are experiencing two problems: infant mortality is disproportionately higher for males than for females, and schools not understanding that males and females mature at different rates, have already begun the negative classification of males, specifically African American male children. The shortage will now magnify.

There is a relationship between the excessive number of Black boys in special education and the 1.5 million African American males that are involved in the penal system. Our concern is that we can intervene as early as infancy if parents and teachers heed the suggestions offered.

Throughout the book I will be offering barometers for parents, teachers and community people to use in monitoring development. We need to have some mechanism to evaluate how well our boys are doing. I propose seven barometers: (1) spiritual development; (2) African identification, specifically their commitment, understanding and appreciation of their race; (3) scholarship and academic achievement, especially in the areas of reading and test taking; (4) self esteem; (5) respect for parents and other adults; (6) the amount of time spent with their friends and its influence on their values; and (7) responsibility for behavior and actions. We don't have to wait until boys are 18-years-old to find out if they're in trouble. We can find out during this stage by using these seven areas.

Spirituality

Studies indicate that little boys that were reared in church have less chance of going to prison. I like that kind of research. We hear so much about what the church is not doing. I think it's important to recognize that even children that are reared in the church and leave when they become older often return to the church, if for no other reason than that's where they were raised.

In this first barometer, we are in trouble if a large number of children, specifically male children, are not developing spirituality. In a later chapter we will look at how parents have different expectations for whether their son or daughter will go to church. The relationship with God will reduce the homicide and self-hatred that exist in the African American community.

Racial Awareness

How well are children developing their African consciousness and awareness? I believe that we can rear Black boys to be men if we can teach African American boys to bond with, identify and understand the lives of Malcolm X and Martin Luther King, Jr. They must have a vision of their history that begins before 1619, and visualize Imhotep designing the first pyramid. I believe our boys are "at risk" when they have a negative image of their history.

Scholarship

We can measure the growth and development of boys by their reading levels. It is essential that boys be taught how to read. It is imperative that we improve the hearing level of our boys and that we use the phonetic approach to reading, which teaches children to attack a word and break it into syllables. We need to provide them with reading materials that are culturally relevant and will enhance their interest. It is also important that adults be mindful that America is a test-taking country, and African American boys must master test-taking skills.

Self-Esteem

In later chapters we are going to provide a comparison between self-esteem and school-esteem. Many educators will have us to believe that our boys have low self-esteem. It may not be that boys have low self-esteem; it may be that because they are placed in classrooms where they are slowerthan the girls (remedial reading), lower-track classes or special education, the schools destroy the boys' self-esteem. In all the other endeavors and activities, engaging in sports, listening to rap music and other social activities, our boys have a high level of self-esteem.

This is a very important area that we need to monitor. Children's self-esteem, but more specifically the school-esteem, is a major factor in their growth and development. We cannot allow boys to simply withdraw from academics out of frustration while they apply themselves and gain confidence in how well they fight, play basketball and make rap records. It is obvious that it may not be our children's low self-esteem but the environment and the insensitivity of educators to the African American male students.

Schools often request that I speak to the male students with the major premise being that the boys lack self-esteem. However, I take the opposite, e.g., that our boys came into the classroom at kindergarten with a high level of self-esteem and that quite possibly the teacher's low expectations and the lack of understanding of the male child and his learning styles may have led to his destruction. We need to monitor our children's self-esteem throughout their academic career.

Peer Pressure

Studies indicate that the greatest influence on children is the peer group, followed by television, home, school and church. Studies also show that home is number one, followed by school, church, peer pressure and television.[9] How well African American families can reduce the amount of time children spend with their friends will also determine how well we develop boys.

Respect for Parents and Elders

I mentioned earlier that "it takes a whole village to raise a child." We have a lot of youths, especially male youths, that are not respecting their parents. In chapter nine we will look at the period between 13 and 18 years of age (adolescence); we have a lot of boys who do not respect their teachers and adults but do not respect their mothers as well. You have mothers who say, "I don't know what to do with him." This loss of control did not begin at thirteen; it began very early. It may have begun in this first period, infancy through nine. There are parents who have lost control of their boys before the age of nine. Many parents, especially mothers, nag their boys, negotiate with their boys, have discussions about when they should wash dishes and when they should empty the garbage, and then wonder how they lost control of their boys. Most believe they lost him when he became a teenager, when they may have lost him before age nine. We are very concerned about this area of our children's growth and development, and we have to instill respect for elders in our boys.

Responsibility

It has often been said that we have a lot of irresponsible men. You cannot be an irresponsible man unless you were allowed to be irresponsible as a boy. Teenage pregnancy is running rampant, and 90 percent of the programs are geared for females, letting the males off the hook. So the question becomes, Who is going to teach Black boys to be responsible? You don't start at sixteen when he's already made a baby. You start very early.

We need parents to teach boys to be responsible for their hygiene, clothes, room and chores. Throughout the book, we will look at other areas of responsibilities, but we believe that early on, at the tender age of two, three and four, we need parents who will teach boys to be responsible in some basic areas.

In the next chapter we will now look at the period between nine and thirteen. I feel that this is the most significant period in Black boys' growth and development. We call this the "Fourth Grade Syndrome."

$\mathscr{C}$HAPTER $\mathscr{T}$HREE

Fourth Grade Failure Syndrome

Since 1974, I have been a national consultant to public and private schools, ranging from preschool through college. My responsibilities are to conduct workshops for teachers and parents and to provide cultural assembly programs for children. It was during my travels that I recognized the conspiracy, often so subtle, mentioned previously. Let me first begin with the innocence of Black boys who bring enthusiasm to the classroom, trust their teachers and are willing to please.

Darryl, who just turned five, has just completed two years of Head Start. His mother informed me that Darryl's only major regret about Head Start is that it lasts only three hours per day. But now Darryl could not wait to see his new teacher, Miss Ford. She smiled at him often and helped him with his shoelaces. I guess the only regret he had about Miss Ford was that she insisted he eat his broccoli, which was not Darryl's favorite food. Darryl loved his classmates and enjoyed singing songs, playing in the sand and listening to stories. Once his classmate Richard was sad about an incident at home, and Darryl was quick to provide instant cheer. Darryl was an eager student. Miss Ford commented, "He asks so many questions." He loved the alphabet and numbers as much as he loved playing with dump trucks in the sand.

Darryl enters the primary division of the neighborhood public school. Many important and tender moments occur in these formative years of kindergarten through third grade. Darryl still sings, but not as loudly and with less enthusiasm. He likes all of his teachers, but each year a little less than before, and none compares with Miss Ford. The alphabet and numbers still interest him, but now the dump truck, his bicycle and his football are his most important possessions.

When I present cultural assembly programs to children, because of the limited seating capacity, I often conduct two or three programs for different grade levels so that all the children will be able to attend. The primary divisions sing and recite louder and seem much happier than the intermediate and upper divisions. My experience has necessitated altering the program for the older division in consideration of their loss of innocence, enthusiasm and trust. Third-grade teachers often ask me what has happened to the Darryls and Richards when they observe their behavior in the upper divisions. I hesitate to answer that question, because I do not consider myself a psychologist but merely a man concerned about the future of his race. I sincerely think that much can be learned by listening to and observing children. I was amazed that teachers with twenty years of experience could not determine what had happened to Darryl and Richard's enthusiasm to learn and trust, and their willingness to please.

I wanted so much to learn from educators. The same holds true for the parents who, in contrast to the teachers, have the child for more than a year. Darryl's mother had witnessed her son's behavior in Head Start, kindergarten, third grade, eighth grade and all grades in between. Unfortunately, the parents seem unable to pinpoint when and what innocence and enthusiasm for learning were lost. If they knew the answer they would be in a better position to alter the trend. I sought the answers from educators and parents because initially I did not know.

The answers were not forthcoming, and my frustration grew with each city where I witnessed the declining achievement of Black boys. I began to respect the subtlety of the conspiracy, and realized that teachers and parents could live with it every day and not be cognizant of it. Again, this is why I focused on African American *boys*; the conspiracy is in its early stages for them and can be treated.

Harry Morgan notes in "How Schools Fail Black Children":

> When blacks enter first grade the stories they create express positive feelings about themselves in the schooling situation, but by the second grade students' stories express "negative imagery of the teacher and school environment," and by the fifth grade the overall feeling expressed by students is that of cynicism.

In other words, upon entering school in primary grades, black children possess enthusiasm and eager interest; however, by fifth grade the liveliness and interest are gone, replaced by passivity and apathy. Primary grades presented a more nurturing environment than intermediate or upper grades. In early childhood education much of the activity is child-teacher centered and child-child interactive. In primary grades, blacks progress and thrive at the same rate as their white counterparts until the third grade syndrome. I found after the third grade, the achievement rate of blacks began a downward spiral which tended to continue in the child's academic career. The classroom environment was transformed from a socially interactive style to a competitive, individualistic, and minimally socially interactive style of learning.[1]

I call this the *"Fourth Grade Failure Syndrome."* It is the poor transition boys make between the primary and intermediate division. Graphically illustrating this phenomenon is this list of twenty male students' Iowa Reading Test scores, indicating their performance at the beginning of the third grade and five academic years later at the end of the seventh grade. My objective was to identify an African American public school with similar demographics matching the income, educational level, and family size of the African American community. In addition, we also had to identify 20 random students who had remained in the same school all five years. I sincerely thank the principal and his staff for providing the sample measurement.[2]

The following is an outline of 20 African American high school males, who took the Iowa Reading Test. This chart shows their performance and that of 20 students chosen at random. Overall, the graph shows how well the students performed over the past five years beginning at the third grade.

Beginning Third Grade Percentile	Ending Seventh Grade Percentile	Reading Progress (Years)
98	35	1.3
97	54	2.7
92	24	2.1
91	68	3.1
81	72	3.9
72	72	3.6
66	59	3.9
63	7	0.7
63	4	0.0
57	39	3.2
47	9	2.1
41	11	2.5
29	12	3.0
21	44	5.6
21	29	4.7
21	17	3.8
18	1	1.3
16	39	4.6
7	30	4.5
5	5	3.2

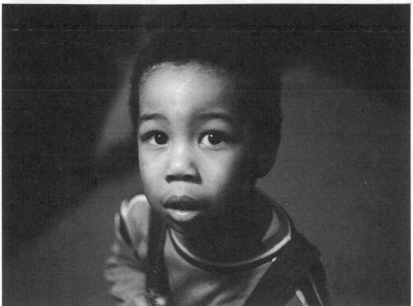

Photo by Kawana Emerson Sherman

The innocence and lively interest typical of the early years change to. . .

35

Photo by Kawana Emerson Sherman

The apathy and limited interest apparent as early as the fourth grade.

Reviewing the scores: fourteen decreased, four improved, and two remained constant. The median beginning percentile was 52, the ending one was 29. The median change in reading was 3.1 years. Only one child was able to improve his reading by five years or more during the same period. There were two children who started at 98 and 92 and dropped to 35 and 24, respectively. We had two geniuses, only to lose them five years later. The boy who started at 63 and dropped to 4 could have stayed at home and watched *Sesame Street!*

Dr. Nancy Arnez, in her book *Implementation of Desegregation as a Discriminatory Process*, reports:

> In 505 school districts in Alabama, Georgia, South Carolina, Mississippi, and Arkansas, which had classes for those labeled as "educable mentally retarded," over 80 percent of the students so labeled were black, although less than 40 percent of the total school district was black.

She further found that, although the biased I.Q test was a major factor producing racial disproportion, the vulnerability of Black children to the labeling process persisted into subsequent classification stages. The study indicated that disproportionately more of the "eligible" Black children were actually recommended for placement into special classrooms, while disproportionately fewer eligible White children were recommended for such placement. A large percentage of the Black children in this study were found to be males.[3]

Additionally, several studies have found that, although African Americans have significantly lower scores, the scores of African American males are demonstrably lower than those of African American females. Bruce Hare, in his sample of ten- and eleven-year olds, further found African American females to have outperformed their male counterparts on measures of achievement orientation. His investigations revealed a hierarchical academic performance structure in which Euro American females were in the middle and African American males at the bottom.[4] The negative consequence for African American males is further highlighted in dropout and pushout statistics. African Americans constitute 17 percent of the total public school enrollment, yet were 21 percent of the dropouts, with African American males constituting the largest category. Thus, the pool of potential college-bound students is effectively reduced.[5] In 2004 there were only 609,000 African American men in college compared to 1.4 million African American females.

The church has not been able to capture the minds of our youth, specifically boys. I hope concerned ministers and church members will look inward and ask themselves why youth, and male youth specifically, have not been attracted. I would also urge them to study the success of the Nation of Islam, specifically the period under the leadership of the Honorable Elijah Muhammad.

Equal Employment Opportunity Commission (EEOC) data reveal that 83 percent of all elementary school teachers were White females, while only 7 percent were African Americans. African American males constituted only 1.2 percent of all teachers. Further, 46 percent of all full-time secondary school teachers were White females.[6] Based on these figures, it could be concluded that a majority of African American males can spend an entire career in the public schools (private schools are not very different) and have very little interaction with an African American male teacher, counselor or administrator.

During the past 30 years, speaking four times a week, my travels have not taken me to many male kindergarten teachers! Men normally enter the picture in the upper grades, when the conspiracy is well under way. Men can usually be found as janitors, security guards, physical education teachers, or administrators. It is a positive experience to find male academic instructors, especially in the primary division. Furthermore, with so few male teachers we can ill afford to lose any to homosexuality.

The complexity of the conspiracy goes beyond the lack of male teachers and a racist/irrelevant curriculum designed to maintain the status quo (training) versus problem solving (education). It also includes the quality and continuity of the teaching staff. Many people are quick to declare public schools incapable of teaching African American children. I have been to many public schools where I witnessed some of the finest educational experiences, public or private. I make it a habit to visit the classrooms after conducting a workshop. In the same public schools that many of us are quick to denounce, I often experience different teaching styles and levels of competence. How can we say public schools cannot educate our children? In one public school I visited, a fifth-grade teacher had 85 percent of her children reading above grade level, but more importantly, had them excited about learning! The problem cannot be easily solved with the condemnation of public schools, racism or the lack of male teachers. To pinpoint the problem we must look at the continuity. The above teacher indicated to me that her students in the fourth grade last year were "turned off" because their prior teacher did not care. She also indicated to me that she feared the choice between the two available sixth-grade teachers boiled down to the lesser of two evils. Parents often tell me how wonderful their children's previous teacher was, but say that during the current year this is not the case. Principals also are quick to mention who are their stalwarts. This scenario is confirmed by the comments from the children about which teachers care. What I learned from these encounters is that all four groups - children, parents, teachers and administrators - recognize quality. Therefore, you are a member of the conspiracy if you allow a child to sit in a classroom one extra day with an unconcerned teacher!

Principals have informed me that they place their "best" teachers, including men, in the upper grades, to maintain order for the most undisciplined children. This Band-Aid approach is part of the conspiracy. It should be obvious that if you stopped the problem in the primary division, you would not have this problem migrating to the upper-grades. When I have shared this observation, the response has been, "But what would we do in the meantime with the upper-grade children?"

The solution then would be to make the staff changes and accept and live with the problem for three years until all those upper grades graduated. The problem is magnified with desegregation, when inner-city schools, in desperation to achieve racial balance allow a disproportionate number of non-Black teachers to teach in the primary division. While this is occurring, some of the better upper-grade teachers of all races become increasingly frustrated, suffer from teacher burnout and contemplate retirement. I cajole more teachers to remain with each passing year.

The problem can be minimized when public school parents realize that the prime difference between them and private school parents is that one pays directly and the other through taxes. Schools still belong to parents, and if parents recognize qualitative differences in their teachers and are not satisfied, they can organize with other parents to either have the teacher removed or keep their children home. As a result, the school will lose money and be forced to remove the teacher. I have also seen concerned, creative teachers develop arrangements with their principals, in which they ensure continuity by placing their most competent teachers in the primary division.

The fastest and greatest influence on most male youth is the streets. There is a direct correlation between age and street time. The transition from the primary division to the intermediate and upper division parallels the increased street time. Street time increases as male youth become older, because most parents spend less time with and give more freedom to their children. Eugene Perkins, in his book *Home is a Dirty Street,* paints the picture:

> Summer mornings never appear to change. They quickly become a part of ghetcolony tradition, a pervasive episode of hopelessness and poverty. What was true yesterday is more than likely to be true today. There are the same decrepit structures basking under the sun with their frayed window shades half drawn, and the odor of hominy grits, fried pork and burnt toast seeping out into the almost death-like air. On hot days one can see fatigued ebony faces protruding out of windows to gain relief from the morning humidity.

And the stenchy alleys covered with broken wine bottles, empty beer cans, urine, and the faces of strayed dogs and unwanted people. And the weary people waiting on street corners to catch the crowded buses which take them to work. And the school aged children who leave home before they have eaten breakfast. And the whimpers of babies who are still hungry for yesterday's shortage of milk. And the dispossessed men who mill in front of taverns waiting to quench their hunger with anything that can help them escape their pain and frustration. And the hustlers, pimps, street men and other social outcasts who serve as models for the young. And the blue squadron flashing down the street or the blaring of a fire truck answering a call of distress. And there are the dirty streets. Always the dirty streets where "ghetcolony" children make their home. A home that has an asphalt floor, tenements for its walls and a door which locks them in from the rest of the world. The streets constitute an institution in the same way that the church, school and family are conceived as institutions. They all have a set of values and norms to govern and reinforce their existence. Of course, the social structure of the street lacks the sophistication these other institutions have. Nevertheless, it is an institution because it helps to shape and control behavior. And it is on the streets where the Black child receives his basic orientation to life. The streets become his primary reference because other institutions have failed to provide him with the essential skills he needs to survive in the "ghetcolony." And for a child to survive the "ghetcolony" he must undergo a rigorous apprenticeship that will enable him to compensate for the lack of guidance from other institutions and adults. He becomes a student of the "asphalt jungle" because that is where he can learn the skills he needs.[7]

When Black children are not compelled to attend school, and often when they are, they usually can be found in the streets. The streets become their text, instructor and subject matter.

The curriculum for this asphalt institution incorporates many of the same courses that are found in the formal school setting: sociology, political science, history, biology and even the physical sciences. However, unlike the school, the courses in the Street Institution are structured around community norms and are most binding on its members.

Its sociology consists of studying the so-called pathology of the ghetto. Political science is learned from the unscrupulous exploits of current politicians, history from years of discrimination and economic deprivation, biology from youths smoking marijuana and having sex in dirty alleys and the physical sciences are taught by learning how to endure elements unfit for human consumption. The theoretical references for the Street Institution reflect how the people actually live and not how others would like them to function. There are no semester breaks or summer vacations, for study in the "ghetcolony" is a continuous cycle which never stops, not even in the face of death.

The values of the Street Institution are shaped from the physical and psychological manifestations of the "ghetcolony." From these manifestations certain lifestyles are created that are exemplified by the instructors of the Street Institution. The instructors consist of hustlers, pimps, street men, militants, gang leaders and working men. And though these men do not have Master's or Ph.D degrees, their credentials have been earned from actual experience and not from the sterile laboratories of formal academic institutions.

A research study commissioned in New Orleans by the public school system and lead by Antoine Garibaldi reviewed the problems facing Black boys. This study shows the levels of declining academic success, and it shows how the problem starts very early. This does not negate my concern about the fourth grade. I am simply saying that Black boys, in spite of harsh problems they experience, do reasonably well. The objective in this chapter is to analyze the factors that are taking place in the lives of Black boys between the ages of nine and thirteen and what we can do to circumvent them.

The significance of this research lies in the area of public policy and intervention. There is a limited amount of human and financial resources. It becomes paramount that all programs are designed to be cost effective. Presently the U.S. government allocates between $18,000 and $38,000 to send someone to prison, $2,300 to Head Start, and $10,000 to send someone to a public college. What is unfortunate is that 85 percent of inmates released from prison return; yet all kinds of studies reinforce the conclusion that Head Start, Chapter 1 and college are effective. If we are serious about solving the problems facing Black boys, then I think we need to understand *when* the best time is to intervene.

As a national consultant to school districts, one of the workshops I enjoy giving the most is entitled "Factors That Contribute to the Fourth Grade Syndrome." I strongly believe that only when we understand what is taking place in the lives of African American boys at the age of nine will we be able to rectify it. The factors that contribute to the decline in African American boys' achievement are:

- a decline in parental involvement
- an increase in peer pressure
- a decline in nurturance
- a decline in teacher expectations
- a lack of understanding of learning styles, and
- a lack of male teachers.

Let's review these factors.

Parental Involvement

As age increases, parental involvement decreases. I don't know who told parents that when children become older they need less of our time rather than more. When I speak to Head Start parents across the country, 80 percent of them are present. At the elementary school level, 30 percent show and in most high schools, parent's meetings aren't even considered.

My wife and I have two sons; we believe that the oldest son needs us more than the youngest. We need parents that will remain involved in their sons' growth and development from infancy through age 18 and beyond. It bothers me that we have so many parents who will attend their children's graduation and such a small number who attend PTA meetings. I call these people graduation parents. Can you imagine instituting a rule that says parents can attend graduation only if they went to, say, an average of six PTA meetings per year?

Peer Pressure

For most children, peer pressure has become the number one influence in their lives, exceeding the influence of parents, teachers and ministers. There are several reasons for this. An obvious one is that our children spend more time with their peers than with parents, teachers and ministers. They want to look and act like their friends, and that's why role models, especially adult Black male role models, are so important. Mothers have often told me that when I say something that they've been telling their sons for years, they finally hear me, and that's because it means more coming from a Black man. My children have also told me that when their friends make comments similar to mine, it means more coming from their friends. Most children emulate people that look like them.

Many people think that all peer pressure is negative. Peer pressure in and of itself is not negative; only when the peer group *is not* reinforcing positive values does it become detrimental. When peer pressure fuses with age and street time, youth become socially aware of the contradictions between what schools teach and the realities of their communities. Disillusioned, they begin to act out negatively.

Although peer pressure has become the greatest influence on many of our children and we will probably never be able to reduce its power, we can infiltrate and incorporate our values into the peer group to reinforce academic achievement. In my earlier book, *To Be Popular or Smart: The Black Peer Group*, I indicated that peer pressure has reached such negative proportions that when our children are doing a good job in school, many of them are teased, especially when a boy is doing well. Now it becomes even harder when they are on the honor roll because they are accused of "acting White." When they speak proper English, they receive the same accusation.

One of the ways we can circumvent this trend is to use the peer group to reinforce academic achievement. The method that can achieve this is called cooperative learning. In a typical classroom of 30 children, teachers normally grade on a curve. Grades are based on the highest score achieved, and distribution ranges are determined accordingly. With cooperative learning, children are divided into groups, and they receive a team grade and an individual grade. It is ironic that African American children, especially boys, do everything together but study. They play ball, listen to records, develop rap songs, get high and hang out together. It is only in the classroom that they are viewed as individuals. Studies also show that Asian students score higher for several reasons, one being that they study together. Cooperative learning is one way to use the peer group to reinforce academic achievement.

The use of cooperative learning will reduce the teacher's need to tell students to be quiet, be still and return to the lesson, because the group reinforces positive behavior. It is very enjoyable to see students on the same team discipline and motivate each other toward academic excellence.

Schools must also realize that they are often guilty of giving mixed and negative messages to children on what activities are to be valued. Schools give more glory to their ballplayers than to their scholars. We give big medals, trophies and pep rallies to the basketball and football teams, and give little certificates, buttons and medals for the winners of the debate, spelling bee and science fair.

Schools must show that they value academic achievement more than athletics and they must also reinforce it with the kind of pomp and glorification that is given to sports.

I remember speaking at a school in Seattle, in the heart of the African American community. There were White male pictures on the wall representing the U.S. Presidents. This really bothered me, the lack of Black male pictures, but it seemed to be OK for the staff teaching these children. Yet, when the children leave the school and go out into the real world, it's the "Silky Floyds" and the "Smooth Reggies" who are selling drugs or simply hanging out on the corner, waiting for life to give them a sense of direction. It is at this period that African American boys begin to wonder, "What is the relevance of learning that Columbus discovered America, that Lincoln freed the slaves, and that Hippocrates was the first doctor? What does this have to do with my survival in my community?" I believe that children have the right to ask why they are learning a particular lesson. I don't think this request is one of defiance

45

or belligerence; I simply feel that if children have to remain in school eight years for an elementary school diploma, four years for a high school diploma, and four years for a bachelor's degree and additional years for a Master's degree and a Ph.D., then they deserve to have some input into what they are learning or at least be able to question why the concepts are important. I also feel that if we can't find some congruency between the lessons and the real world, then it's worth considering a change in the curriculum.

Boys - No Longer "Cute"

To some, as boys become older, they become more aggressive and hostile, disciplinary programs. It is amazing to me how little Christopher at three, five and seven years of age was viewed as a nice, sweet, innocent little boy, but now that Christopher has become nine, 11 and 13, he's viewed as being rough, rugged and aggressive and is being recommended for suspension.

Many teachers and parents, during the first period between infancy through nine, use their size to discipline. They simply are larger than the boys. From the fourth grade on, children, specifically most boys, become taller than the teachers. They can look adults directly in the eye and as they become older they will probably look down at them. Teachers and parents are no longer able to discipline male students with their height. For the insecure or intimidated parent or teacher, having to look a child in the eye and not back down becomes a serious problem. This situation requires a parent or teacher who is very confident and assertive. This adult gives very clear messages about who is in control in the classroom as well as in the home. I am reminded of the stories of the good old days when a four-foot-one mother who was 70-years-old could tell her seven-foot 30-year-old son, "I brought you in this world and I'll take you out."

I am very much aware of the limitations that schools have had placed upon them about not being able to spank children, but adults who give very clear, assertive messages are still effective in the classroom. Parents need to tell children that any adult that they come in contact with is to be respected.

46

Low Teacher Expectations

Numerous studies by Wilbur Brookover, Ron Edmonds and Antoine Garibaldi indicate that some teachers lower their expectations based on the race, income, gender and appearance of the child. For Black boys, the combination of being African American, male, low-income and poorly dressed puts them "at risk."

This is a very popular term, "at risk." Most people who use the term tend to blame the victim. When we use the term, we need to look at the institutions and the factors that caused this child to be at risk. The study that was done in New Orleans indicated that 60 percent of the teachers did not believe that African American boys were going to college. I reiterate that teacher expectations are the most important factor in academic achievement. You do not measure a school by its facilities, or the race of the student population, but by teachers' expectations. I believe that what teachers *see* in the child is what they produce *out* of the child. If teachers see in Black boys future engineers, computer programmers and doctors, if they see Benjamin Carson and Walter Massey, then they will produce those kinds of practitioners and scholars.

Children learn best when they are given feedback and reinforcement. Studies indicate that low-achieving Black boys are given very few clues and little feedback when answering questions incorrectly. Research indicates that girls receive approximately three minutes to correct the wrong answer. I believe that low-achieving African American boys can also answer questions correctly with this kind of prodding, nurturance and attention.

In the fourth grade, more abstract thinking is expected. The classroom becomes less child-centered in that more homework is allocated and less movement is allowed. There is more left-brain methodology and less right-brain lesson planning, i.e., stories, pictures, fine arts and artifacts.

If in the first period between infancy and nine boys are disproportionately placed in remedial reading and special education, then the fourth grade and this whole intermediate period make the final decision on who's going to college, lucrative careers and businesses.

Lack of Male Teachers

Up until the fourth grade, African American boys probably have not had the opportunity to experience an African American male teacher. I was very fortunate, when I was growing up at a very critical age and in the fourth grade, to have had a Black male teacher by the name of Mr. Payne. I believe that in order to *be* a Black man you need to *see* Black men. I indicated earlier that the present population of Black male teachers is only 1.2 percent. The overall shortage of Black teachers will become more acute for Black males by the year 2020. Again, I ask the question of the larger community: How are we going to develop Black boys to be men if they have not seen one? Why do we not want to educate our children?

When America had an extreme shortage of math and science teachers, schools altered their criteria and qualifications and allowed professionals in other fields such as engineers and accountants to teach. Provisions were made to provide the training course work and pedagogy. Many private schools have successfully used this approach. I believe that the same urgency, if not a greater one, exists in the lack of African American teachers.

It's obvious that the present power structure does not value African American male teachers as much as I do, so it is up to the African American community to put pressure on school districts to come up with programs and provisions that will increase the number of African American teachers, specifically male teachers.

There is a movement afloat in many states to entice younger students into considering teaching. In Iowa, they are working with sixth-through eighth-grade students, promising scholarships if they agree to teach. I commend these efforts, and we need more incentives like this one.

The long-term solution is to have role models inspire our students, especially Black males, at a very young age to consider teaching. Secondly, we need to have institutions that will provide scholarships to students who promise to teach. Several private schools have responded to these suggestions. These institutions went to the streets, community colleges and other places and recruited Black males who had potential. Now they are reaping the benefits of having some very positive Black males in their classrooms.

I am very much aware of the problems that may occur from unions that often want to maintain the status quo but we need creative administrators who will respond, as Malcolm X used to say, "by any means necessary." If we cannot increase the number of African American males in schools on a full-time basis, then every effort should be made by schools to implement the program, "A Hundred Black Men." I am pleased to see the growth of this program in cities across the country. I just do not believe that 100 Black men in Chicago, New York, Los Angeles, Washington or Atlanta will solve the problems that we are currently experiencing. We need them for each *school*, not just each *city*.

Two programs that are doing an excellent job of intervening at the right time with the proper strategy are in Waterloo, Iowa and Houston, Texas. The program in Waterloo matches 50 to 75 at risk Black boys in fourth grade to Black male role models who will spend four to six hours a week interacting with the children. In-service training is provided for the teacher, mentor and parents. I had the fortunate opportunity to speak at a ceremony where 75 men placed kente cloth on the shoulders of 75 boys. The men made a commitment to remain in contact with the boys through their eighteenth birthday.

The program was funded for only one to three years, and like most governmental programs, just when the bugs and idiosyncrasies were being removed from the operation, the money stopped. We need to begin to build programs the way we built the pyramids. Our ancestors built the pyramid of Gizeh in 2700 B.C. This later became one of the seven wonders of the world. We built pyramids that lasted more than 5,000 years, but our programs die in three.

I was also impressed that the program was in Waterloo, not in New York, Chicago or Los Angeles. My only desire is to institute more programs of this caliber. Another program that I greatly respect is the Fifth Ward Enrichment Program in Houston. The combination of role models going into the schools and providing counseling and tutoring during the school day and providing recreational and informational sessions in the evenings and on weekends has been very successful. Most schools do not have counselors at the elementary school level and have an inadequate number at the high school level. The ratio of students to counselor is something like 300-500. It has become obvious that very little counseling is taking place and children who are at risk, specifically Black boys, need counseling before high school. We need more adults, specifically African American males, to consider counseling and tutoring our youth.

If we cannot do a better job of developing African American boys to their fullest potential, then I recommend an extreme solution — the design of a Black male classroom .

I made this recommendation in 1985. There have been many challenges from ACLU, NOW, Title IX, etc. Two decades later, the government, ACLU, NOW and others realize the effectiveness of single gender classrooms. I encourage you to visit the National Association of Single Sex Public Education website to read about the excellent results.

The major components of the Black classroom would include:

- Black Male Teachers
- Twenty to Twenty-Four Students
- Cooperative Learning
- SETCLAE Curriculum
- Physical Education
- Nutritious Daily Meals
- Science Lab
- Martial Arts Training
- Phonics
- Musical Instruments
- Whole-brain Lesson Plans and Tests
- Math Word Problems
- Junior Business League
- Corporate Sponsors for Summer Employment
- Academic Contests and Assemblies
- Monthly Parent Meetings
- Chess

SETCLAE represents the kind of classes and schools we would like all of our children to experience, but especially African American male children. Our staff would train the teachers on expectations, learning styles, SETCLAE, cooperative learning and all the components that would best socialize our boys. This kind of setting would no longer place Black boys in the tenuous position of being compared to female students who have matured faster and of being taught exclusively by female teachers.

This type of classroom would correct the problem of Black boys not being taught by an African American male teacher. The high energy that boys naturally have would be channelled into daily physical education and martial arts. Boys' competence in handling objects and artifacts would be used in the science lab. Music would be used to teach mathematics. This classroom will teach critical thinking skills. It will use word problems and establish a junior business league, which will try to show the relevance of the classroom to the streets. It should be amazing, to everyone that the same boy who failed math in a classroom is able to measure kilos and grams for drugs and to convert it to dollars and cents on the street.

The major objection to the all-Black male classroom is that it's discriminatory and it harkens back to segregated classrooms. What my detractors don't understand, though, is that with 75 percent or more African American boys in special education and remedial classes, classrooms are already segregated, Nobody seems to object to that. Since the boys are already in a separate class, why don't we take advantage of the opportunity -- for them as well as for high-achieving male students. I'm glad that there are some creative and committed superintendents and administrators who are now pursuing this classroom and investigating how legal problems can be avoided.

I am pleased that the government has become more acceptable to single gender classrooms and schools. These programs have been able to withstand the legal litmus test of Title IX legislation because we are also providing single gender classrooms and schools for females. Thurgood Marshall School in Seattle reported a 78 percent decline in suspensions and a six stanine increase in test scores with the male classroom. Other schools have experienced similar results with the male classroom or school.

I also recommended at the NABSE convention a moratorium on special education placements for the African American male child, except in extreme cases. The numbers indicate that there is something wrong with the way we are classifying children. When 17 percent of public school children are African American, but 41 percent of the children are placed in special education and 85 percent of those Black children are male, something is wrong with the *system*, not the *children*.

It is also imperative that we understand that five percent of the teachers make 30 percent of the referrals. A better solution would be to mandate in-service training or institute a policy that would allow for the removal of such teachers. Unfortunately, teachers have a union and African American boys do not. I have chosen to represent the Black boys' union. We need more adults to stop this onslaught.

In Detroit, a pilot program brings the special education resources to the children rather than removing the child from the mainstream classroom. Many schools have become trigger-happy, e.g., they pull children out to receive increased funding to their school district. This is not totally the schools' fault. Schools receive additional money based on how many students are classified at the upper and lower extremes. Consequently, schools receive additional funds for having gifted students or special education students, not average students.

One of the most important meetings of a child's life is the one that determines whether the child will be placed into special education. The principal, teacher, social worker and psychologist will be in attendance. In most schools, once the recommendation has been made by the teacher, the school worker, psychologist and principal will concur. A low-income single parent may become very intimidated when meeting with four educated people who are all recommending that the child be placed in special education. My concern is that the aggregate figures in special education are the result of each of these individual meetings. This one meeting may contribute to the large number of Black boys who do not receive a high school diploma, do not go on to college, end up in prison and do not become responsible husbands and fathers. We cannot afford to lose any more boys to special education.

A study published in *Harvard Educational Review* indicated that special education may not be all that special, except for the fact that African American children are placed there *more* than anyone, stay *longer* than anyone else, and don't return to the main classroom at their appropriate *grade level*. What makes special education special? How do we evaluate special education?

Again, parents, I cannot stress enough that you have to meet teachers where they are. If a lack of understanding exists between the classroom teachers and Black male students, then we must develop programs and literature that will help educators understand how children learn. We must consider placing a moratorium on special education placement. We must increase the number of Black male teachers or design a Black male classroom. And parents must increase the amount of study and quiet time at home; they must reduce the amount of time that their children spend watching television, talking on the telephone, listening to the radio or record player and playing Nintendo. During this period of preadolescence (9 through 13), we need parents who will listen to their sons read. Parents should not accept illiteracy in their preadolescent children. Unfortunately, many parents are not aware that their 13-year-old son is reading at a primary level.

It is during preadolescence when many adults have growing concerns about the self-esteem of their children. Many people feel that Black boys suffer from low self-esteem. We have indicated that self-esteem is very complex and that a person may be very confident and have a healthy dose of self-esteem in one endeavor and may be very intimidated and hesitant in another. I take the position that Black boys do not suffer from low self-esteem outside of the classroom, and are very confident with their friends, girlfriends and in many social activities. When Black boys are placed in lower-track classes such as remedial reading and special education, are labeled hyperactive and are not given high expectations, their self-esteem plunges in the classroom. It is also very significant that African American boys who may have been destroyed in the classroom somehow find ways to feel good about themselves within Black culture. Gangs and rap records are expressions of this phenomenon.

Finally, let's discuss the significance that *sports* has on the African American male, especially at the impressionable ages of nine through thirteen.

In speaking to students across the country, I often ask the boys to share their career goals with me. More than half the group will tell me that they plan to go to the NBA, NFL, or Major League Baseball. Because I am a strong advocate of developing self-esteem, the last thing I want to do is to destroy someone's dream of becoming a professional ballplayer. However, I do attempt to make the students aware that the odds are one million to 35 that they will achieve this objective, and that the odds are better that they will become engineers, computer programmers, or doctors.

Every effort should be made to try to reduce the allure of money making sports. I have observed schools where 200 athletes have tried out for ten athletic teams — basketball, football, baseball, wrestling, swimming, track, gymnastics and others. One hundred students tried out for the basketball team, 25 for football, 25 for baseball and the other 50 students tried out for the remaining seven sports. I try to convince youth they have a much better chance making the swimming or track team than making the basketball team. This may be an excellent opportunity to secure a scholarship and develop a career. Youth, especially between the ages of nine and thirteen, don't care about odds. They believe that they will be the one out of a hundred on their high school team and one out of a million going to the NBA.

In conclusion, we must assess how well our boys are doing against our seven barometers that we are using to monitor their growth and development: spirituality, racial awareness, scholarship, school, self-esteem, peer pressure, respect for authority and responsibility. We don't lose our boys instantaneously; we lose them when they stop growing spiritually, when they become cynical and disdain reading about their history, as their reading levels and math scores begin to lag behind the national average. We lose our boys when they begin to lack confidence in their ability to successfully manage school; they no longer volunteer to read aloud, go up to the board or answer questions. They no longer volunteer to be in public programs.

We must monitor the influence of the peer group. This is a volatile period when boys may become involved with gangs. It is our responsibility to monitor the time and influence that the peer group has on our children.

In *To Be Popular or Smart: The Black Peer Group*, I indicated that good parents *know* their children's friends, *invite* them over, *program* their activities, and make sure they *check* back every so often. Children who leave home at one o'clock in the afternoon on Saturday should be seen before ten and eleven o'clock that night. We must monitor whether or not our boys are respecting authority, in the home, school, church and community.

Finally, in the preadolescent period between nine and 13, our boys should become more responsible managing money and studying.

The next chapter will explore how successful parents are in teaching their sons to be responsible.

The fourth grade is the most pivotal time in African American male development.

CHAPTER FOUR

Developing Responsibility in Black Boys

The most frequent response I received upon releasing *Countering the Conspiracy to Destroy Black Boys* was that more should have been written about teaching Black boys to be responsible. The revised edition declared, "Some mothers raise their daughters and love their sons." Over the years I have observed that when it comes to their sons, *some* mothers have low expectations for academic excellence and seldom assign household chores. On the contrary, girls are expected to perform well in school as well as share a good load of the e.g. housework. This double standard reinforces the stereotype that household chores and academics are for girls only. Further, it serves to create conflicting expectations in adult male-female relationships: she has learned to be responsible and expects him to be too. Not only has he not learned, he expects her to do all the cooking, cleaning, washing, ironing, homework with the children, etc.

The present day mother-son relationship reflects the history of the African American experience. Mothers can be heard referring to their "littleman of the house" or negatively to that "no-good boy" who's "just like your no-good father." My concern in my book, *Motivating and Preparing Black Youth for Success*, was parents who work to give their children everything but become annoyed when their children lack drive and enthusiasm. Mothers who give everything and allow their sons to live at home indefinitely do not help their children grow up. There are mothers who buy their sons expensive gym shoes, stereos and leather bags while providing free room, board and meals indefinitely.

I ask mothers in my workshops for their reasons why some "raise their daughters and love their sons." Here are some of their responses and my comments:

1) **Mothers are not supported by fathers in encouraging domestic responsibility.**
This response applies to less than four percent of the households where the men still reside with their children. I understand a mother's concern. Parenting is much more effective when there is mutual agreement. When the father does not subscribe to this school of thought, a mother's appeal will be less effective.

2) **Mothers lack knowledge of masculinity.**
Many boys still believe domestic activities are feminine and may lead to homosexuality. A single parent once told me her son did not want to wash dishes the previous night after dinner because washing dishes was feminine. The next evening, the parent was going to serve her son on the same dirty plate used previously. The son washed his plate, not because it was masculine or bordering on femininity, but because he wanted his food on a clean plate.

3) **Mothers use their sons to replace an absent husband.**
How many mothers have told their son, You are the man of the house? Can a nine-year-old boy be a man? Have mothers come to rely on their strong son to do the physical work around the house? While I am in favor of boys doing whatever is necessary, I am concerned that mothers, consciously or unconsciously, use this work, to keep their sons with them permanently.

4) **Mothers hold their daughters to a higher standard.**
The double standard that exists is not healthy for boys' development and is disastrous for future adult male-female relationships. When daughters are taught to cook, sew, clean, visit libraries and attend church and are expected to be on the honor roll, while boys are allowed to play basketball all evening after school, never visit libraries or church, cannot boil a hot dog and have never been on the honor roll, the Black family has a very serious problem.

5) **Mothers protect their sons from racism.**
Historically, Black mothers shielded their sons to keep them from being lynched. This is very complex historically and

The persons most likely to teach Black boys to be responsible are Black mothers.

---

contemporarily. I don't know if the present-day mother consciously thinks about lynching when she lowers her expectations for her son and does not push him to society's limit, when she overcompensates her efforts to help her daughter to reach her full potential. If mothers don't believe their sons will be able to become self-sufficient in this racist society, she will rear him to become more dependent on her.

The question then becomes, Who is going to teach Black boys to be responsible in White America? Black men? Female teachers? Ministers? Peers? Television? Radio? Bosses? The extended family? Athletic Coaches? Fathers? Mothers? I believe the motive for the conspiracy is White male supremacy. If you think the only reason for our problem is because of somebody else, you have given them a compliment they do not fully deserve. You can blame White men for a portion of the problem, but White men do not determine if our boys wash dishes and clean up their rooms. I can be critical of Black mothers only to a degree; the major indictment is on those Black men, specifically Black fathers, who began their jaunt toward irresponsibility by making a baby they refused to care for.

I have observed different responses from unemployed fathers. Some fathers cry in their misery and make the matter worse with abuse, neglect and crime. Other fathers in the same circumstances will sell papers or peanuts or provide landscaping or garbage removal services. Should Black men and women accept these narrow gender roles or should they understand that even while unemployed, men can help their children with homework, teach them the beauty of being Black and a Christian, and also assist their wives with housework? Until we redefine manhood and limit the psychological effect of welfare, we will continue to observe the phenomenon of boys making babies.

What is "being responsible?" Webster defines it as accepting obligation, being answerable and accountable. Why are some Black men so irresponsible? I am reminded of a food co-op I was a member of. We would purchase the food from a large distribution facility at 3 a.m. I was a weekly regular, and we had rotating assistants. One brother in particular was always late or absent. As I pondered his circumstances, I observed a chaotic family and an unpredictable lifestyle; he simply did not have the internal fabric to be responsible and consistent. It was often hard for me to accept this, because my father worked evenings but called the house at exactly 8 p.m. every night of my childhood. I thought all men were like my father. I now understand that responsibility must be taught early. I am tired of Black women complaining about Black men being irresponsible when they have the best opportunity to correct the problem with their sons. I repeat, responsible men are born in boyhood. Remember, our little boys will be someone's future husband and father.

Here is a general list of tasks, chores, character developers, etc., that should be reinforced on a daily basis.

personal hygiene	toys and equipment
clothes	schedule
room	sexual activity
household chores	law
siblings	residence
allowance	health
studies	race
	God

Who is going to teach Black boys good hygiene and proper grooming? Who is going to insure that Black boys do not play in their good clothes and hang them up after school? When will Black boys be expected to make their beds daily and clean their rooms periodically? Who is going to make Black boys wash dishes, mop, vacuum, dust, sew and cook? When will Black boys be expected to take care of their siblings in preparation for fatherhood?

Who will teach their sons how to manage their allowance, so that they won't be like so many men who carry a wad of money in their pocket and cannot explain what happened to it at the end of the week or month? In our house, both boys are required to save a portion of their allowance each week; at the end of the year they have an option of spending it or saving a portion, which we will match and invest. Two lessons are taught; first, what they save each week is very small and could buy very little, but money accumulated throughout the year amounts to a significant sum and promotes the value of saving. Secondly, a matching grant incentive and investment teaches how money can work for them.

Who is going to teach Black boys to do their homework as soon as they come home from school, music and television off? Who is going to teach them to be responsible for their grades and actions in school? When are Black boys going to learn to take one toy outside at a time and always bring it back in before taking out another? When are they going to be taught to put their toys in one location in their room, and how to avoid breaking them? Who is going to teach their sons to be punctual about time commitments and class schedules?

When are Black boys going to be responsible for their sexual promiscuity? A documentary titled *The Vanishing Black Family* that portrayed a brother who was irresponsible, many people thought he was an actor. He said, "Making babies is like a piece of art; you lay back and look at your work." There are parents who know their son has impregnated a sister on the block but do not hold him accountable. In the same documentary the sister said, "I want the baby because I want someone to love me, but I don't want to marry the father because he can't even take care of himself." Our society, specifically families,

Who is going to teach Black boys to do their homework as soon as they come home from school?

---

have a double standard on this issue. Statements such as "boys will be boys — all boys have some dog in them" and "boys have to soak a few wild oats" all reinforce boys' feeling that they can do whatever they want sexually.

Ninety percent of all teenage pregnancy programs service females. When you hear the phrase *teenage pregnancy,* most people think *girls.* My studies still confirm that it takes consenting parties of both genders to produce a baby. I applaud programs like Project Alpha, the Urban League and the National Fatherhood Initiative for providing concrete programs and counseling for the "other party." While we need to commend these and other programs holding Black boys accountable, the first level of responsibility still resides in the home. When are parents going to hold their sons accountable for their sexual behavior? I believe there is a direct correlation between a boy being allowed to be irresponsible about his hygiene, clothes, room, household chores, siblings, money, studies, toys, activities and schedule to his sex life. If a boy has been irresponsible about everything else, why should we expect anything different in his sexual behaviors? Another book is needed to explain why girls are also sexually irresponsible.

Most adults, especially mothers, are not comfortable talking to their sons about sex. Unfortunately, most boys learn inaccurate sexual information on the streets. Parents may timidly drop a book on their 16 year-old son's bed, saying, "Let me know if you have any questions." Or you get "open minded" parents who accept that "boys will be boys," or are "highly sexed," as the brother in the *Vanishing Family* documentary stated, and give their sons an unlimited supply of condoms.

Research shows that youth, specifically those labelled "high risk," become sexually active at 12 or 13 years of age. This is important, because most homes, schools and churches provide counseling for youth 16 years and older. The fundamental question is, what is the objective of our counseling? Moral guidance? Dispensing contraceptives? Many parents and institutions have dropped the first line of defense, which is moral responsibility. The second step is accepting the act but protecting yourself against pregnancy. I often tease my workshop audience on teenage pregnancy by declaring, "I can stop teenage pregnancy if you can stop teenage sex!" Our sad state of affairs results from a lack of moral responsibility, inadequately preparing our children on the use of contraceptives and not holding them accountable for their "piece of art." My father always told me, "If you make it, you will take care of it." I believed him. I actually thought that if a girl's parents came to my house and convinced my parents that I was the father of her child, my school plans and savings would have been altered. This kind of background makes a boy think twice about his actions. My father also said, "Welfare didn't make it, and welfare will not take care of it."

The next area of responsibility is the law. Schools and the larger society operate on rules; if the rules are broken there are direct consequences. When there are no rules at home and no repercussions, it is difficult for all youth to understand, especially Black boys who spend a disproportionate amount of time on the streets. Discipline is the number one problem in elementary schools, and many teachers say, "How can I discipline them when their parents don't?" Who is going to teach Black boys to respect rules, the law and authority? Again, I refer to my father who told me early on, "If you get caught breaking the law and get locked up, don't even think about calling." (I knew my mother would get me out, whatever the reason.) Please note, I am very much aware of police brutality and the large number of brothers who are in jail for no other reason than racism and lack of money. I am referring to those unquestionable violations, such as rape, burglary and murder, where parents will still plead in defense of their sons.

Who is going to hold Black boys accountable for becoming employed? People have told me their parents said, "You will either go to school or get a job, but you are not going to lay up in this house." Granted, institutional racism in America confirms Sidney Wilhelm's prediction in *Who Needs the Negro?* Alvin Toffler, in *The Third Wave,* describes the White power brokers' disdain and disregard for Black labor. White suburbia has help wanted signs in numerous fast-food franchises, but many of the jobs are simply inaccessible to Black teenagers, and their minimum wage are inadequate for heads of households. I mentioned earlier that despite these conditions, some brothers will sell newspapers or peanuts before selling drugs or "pimping" off their mother or "lady." I remembered when I could not find work in high school, I volunteered to work with an electrical firm to learn how to be an electrician. They first questioned my desire to volunteer, then felt sorry for me and gave me bus money, and eventually gave me a little spending money. But more importantly, I learned the basics of being an electrician.

Who is going to teach Black boys to be responsible for their education, employment and overall skill development? If Black boys are allowed to stay with their parents indefinitely without contributing to the household financially, and do not attend school or develop skills, how will they ever learn responsibility? The relationship some boys have with their mothers parallels the parasitic relationships some sisters have with welfare. In each case, the authority figures expects nothing from the dependent, and consequently, the person becomes more irresponsible and dependent.

When are Black boys going to learn the relationship between diet and health? Who is going to prevent our boys from smoking cigarettes at age 11, creating a lifetime addiction and potentially premature death? Life expectancy tables show the following life expectancies:

European women	79 years
African American women	75 years
European men	75 years
African American men	69 years[1]

Black men often die before receiving their first Social Security check. Who is going to take Black boys for their annual medical and dental checkup?

Lastly, who is going to teach Black boys to be committed to the liberation of Black people and to place God first in their lives? In my experience providing cultural and religious programs for youth, I observe different standards for sons and daughters. Why should we be surprised when we see more women involved in cultural and religious activities when as children, the pattern was already being molded? Many parents require their daughters to attend Black and religious events, but leave it optional for their "little man of the house."

In conclusion, developing responsibility in Black boys is essential if we want responsibility from Black men. Responsibility starts early. The relationship between some mothers and sons needs an honest assessment. It also has implications not only for adult male-female relations but also for the associations boys have with their female teachers. Often boys think the way they negotiate, plead, rap and manipulate their mothers can also be used with their female teachers, girlfriends, and later, their wives. The next chapter will explore further the relationship between mothers and sons and what are her major concerns developing him into manhood.

Photo by Kawana Emerson Sherman

"Solving the problems of Black boys may eliminate the problems of future men."

Chapter Five

Mothers and Sons

It had been a beautiful Saturday afternoon and a great game. Before leaving the park, a few of us decided to stop at the restroom. While I waited outside for my nine-year-old son, I couldn't help but overhear a conversation an African American woman was having with her son. He looked to be about four or five years of age. Basically, she was explaining to him how to use the restroom. She seemed to be well educated and very accomplished. Sometimes I like to look at people and see how much I can learn about them in three to five minutes. My first impressions were confirmed while we waited for our boys. We chitchatted about how pleased we were that our home team had won. It was ironic, she said, that while today she cheered for the home team, soon she would be traveling to the opposing team's city to represent her client as their attorney.

My son came out, but before I could say my good-byes, she asked if I would mind going in to see what was holding up her son. "All he had to do was urinate," she said. No problem, I said, and told my son to stay next to her. I went into the restroom and looked for the boy by the long row of urinals. He was nowhere to be found. I was just about to leave when I saw him coming out of one of the enclosed stalls. I asked him why was he using the toilet when he could have used the urinal. He said, "We don't have one of those at home, and I don't know how to use it." I was amazed. Using the urinal was something I took for granted. At that point I began to wonder if he was the only male child in America who had this problem, or if there were other children, especially African American male children, without a significant male influence in their lives? I walked the child out of the washroom and explained to his mother what had happened. I then asked her if I could take him back inside and give him a five-minute class in Urinology 101.

For the last two decades, I have devoted my life to the empowerment of African American people, with a strong concentration on the development of the African American male. I raise many questions, analyze issues and look for trends that both positively and negatively affect the development of African American male children. The incident at the park sent out a red alert to me. What other rites of passage and learning experiences were African American boys missing under the guidance of African American women who were doing their level best?

The Lord had more for me that Saturday as he prepared me to write this next book. That evening I was scheduled to speak at an awards banquet. The awardees were freshmen entering college. They were spending the entire summer in a science camp sponsored by the local college. The purpose of the camp was to increase the number of African Americans in the sciences. As I spoke, I mentioned how much I respected their work. Then I gave them the cold facts: only two percent of the doctors and one percent of the engineers in America are African American. I teased my audience and asked them how many Asians play in the NBA.

There were 49 awardees at the program, 35 African Americans and 14 Latinos. There were six males, four African Americans and two Latinos. Two of the four African American males would fit the description of "nerd." One was overweight, seemed to possess homosexual tendencies and acted very childish. The young man who introduced me looked like an eighth-grader rather than a freshman entering college. He seemed to possess some physical impairments, including a visual problem that made it difficult for him to read his introduction.

I thought about the sisters in the audience and the numerical disparity between them and the brothers, and I wondered what they were going to do when it came time to select a mate. In my book *The Power, Passion and Pain of Black Love,* I mentioned that if a sister has a BA degree, she has a 10 percent less chance of getting married. After completing one year of graduate school it becomes 15 percent and if she earns a Masters degree, a Ph.D. or makes over $40,000 a year, then it becomes 19 percent. At the banquet there were 31 females to a mere four African American males. The other two young men were tall, suave and athletic. I was very glad to see them. I later learned that one of them came from a highly dysfunctional family. His mother was a crack-head and his father was the latest boyfriend in her life.

I began to reflect and juxtapose what I saw today. There was the middle-income African American female attorney whose son did not know how to use a urinal. And there was the African American male college freshman, the product of a crack-head mama and an absent father, who had successfully completed a six-week intensive science camp. It became obvious that a child's final destination in life transcends race, class and gender.

In this chapter on the relationship between mothers and their sons - an issue which transcends class - we will examine some of the many challenges facing mothers as they attempt to rear their male children.

I am reminded of a conversation I had with a middle-income African American woman. Her son was having problems in school and she was having difficulty resolving them. Ironically, she was a teacher in the very same school district. Her third-grade son claimed that his teacher was making derogatory comments about him. She wrote a letter to the teacher in order to get her side of the story, as well as to share her son's comments, and she requested a return letter. Three weeks later, having received no response, she called the school and attempted to either talk with the teacher or arrange for a mutually convenient time to meet. No response. This is one of the same schools, no doubt, that encourages parents' involvement and support.

The third time she called she did not ask for the teacher; she asked for the principal. She told the principal that if she did not have the teacher call within 24 hours, she would "be in school first thing tomorrow morning." My friend has always believed that the lack of parental involvement is the reason why our children suffer academically. Teachers who have children, especially male children, in regular public schools (vs. gifted or "magnet" programs) have a unique understanding of how challenging it is to fight school districts. She told me that the teacher finally called her late that night and they scheduled a meeting for the following morning.

As she waited in the school office for the teacher to arrive, she overheard a conversation between someone who she thought was a low-income parent and the school clerk who apparently thought the parent was not important enough to warrant a meeting with either the teacher or the principal. My friend said that for the first time in her life she realized all that she and her low-income sister had in common. Although one was educated while the other was a dropout, one made over $40,000 while the other was probably on AFDC (Aid to Families with Dependent Children). One was wearing an expensive fur coat while the other was wearing an old handy-down coat, and one was wearing a designer dress while the other wore blue jean cutoffs, in the final analysis, they both were trying to negotiate with a school system on behalf of their sons. Having an extensive vocabulary or lacking one made no difference. They both sat there at the mercy of a school system that held the future of their most prized possession, the man-child.

This chapter is a response to the large number of letters I receive on a regular basis from mothers nationwide who have either read one of the earlier volumes of *Countering the Conspiracy to Destroy Black Boys,* heard me speak on the subject or have been referred by someone who thinks that I may be able to provide some direction. I would like to share with you some of the more heart-wrenching letters I have received. The names have either been altered or deleted for anonymity. I think it is imperative that we understand the concern, pain and anguish that mothers are experiencing as they attempt to raise their sons alone. This first letter is from Ms. Johnson.

Dear Dr. Kunjufu:

You don't know me, but I have read most of your books on Black boys and I was hoping that you could give me some advice concerning my son. Last week, I attended a staff meeting that was very intimidating. I was the only African American in the conference room. Seated around the table was a principal, psychologist, social worker and teacher, who all used a lot of acronyms - BD, ADD, EMR and EMH. It made me feel uncomfortable in the meeting, besides the fact that I was the only African American. They were there before I arrived and it seemed as if their minds were already made up when they recommended that my child be placed in a BD classroom, because he has been evaluated as being hyperactive and suffers from an attention deficit disorder. The first question posed to me was, Did I drink or use drugs, specifically during pregnancy? What really baffled me about that question was this child was almost on the honor roll last year and my personal background had not been an issue. I told them that I drink a little beer and that was the extent of my drinking. They went on to say that they felt that my child had difficulties following instructions, completing his assignments, was often restless in class, and was easily distracted. They thought the drug Ritalin would help reduce some of this nervous energy. Dr. Kunjufu, I don't know what to do.

Should I agree to have my child placed in special education? I asked them if I could at least have a week to make the decision. I really felt that the decision had already been made before I had arrived. I simply don't know what to do. Please call me tonight.

First of all, it was essential to let her know that I cared, that I appreciated the respect that she had for my work and that I felt limited in what I could do because of the distance that separated us. I did, however, suggest that she utilize the resources of her local chapters of the National Association of Black Social Workers (NABSW), Black Psychologists, the National Association of Black School Educators (NABSE), the National Black Child Development Institute, a local teacher's advocacy group or a sympathetic legal aid organization.

Whenever I talk to mothers in this kind of predicament, I refer them to Countering the Conspiracy to Destroy Black Boys, in which I stress the fact that parents have rights. For example, a child cannot be placed in special education without the signature of a guardian unless the school is willing to pursue a hearing or arbitration. Many times parents are not aware of their rights. I suggested to this mother that at the next meeting she have a representative with her to balance the racial disparity. It's also good for emotional support. As the child had almost made the honor roll in the previous grade, I also suggested that she seek the support of her son's former teachers. Unfortunately, some schools operate like police departments, in that the bond among staff supersedes what is best for the child.

Principals should critically evaluate their teachers before placing the entire onus on the child. Most principals are aware that 20 percent of their staff make 80 percent of the referrals for special education. The problem may be with the teacher rather than the student. I then asked the parent, if she knew how long they thought the special education class would be needed and what criteria they were using to measure success. I try to point out to parents that presently there is no evaluation instrument to measure the effectiveness of special education.

Before she met again with the faculty and administration, I suggested that the mother honestly assess her son's behavior by answering the following questions:

✓ How well do you really know your child?
(Games like Checkers, Dominoes, Scrabble and Concentration can help you assess the ability of your child to be focused and follow instructions.)

✓ Does your child have a short or long attention span?

✓ How much TV does your child watch?

✓ What kind of TV programs does your child watch?

The better you know your child, the better you can negotiate the system on his behalf.

I encourage parents to videotape their child if they can. I'll never forget the mother who did follow this suggestion. Her child had been assessed with an attention deficit disorder, but the tape showed, without a shadow of a doubt, a child who was focused during his playtime.

I give mothers a list of questions that they need to ask their sons' teachers. Many schools know how to avoid the major issues when they dialogue with parents. One of the favorite lines that teachers give to parents is, "Your son has the potential, but he is not working to his capacity." If the teacher had told the parent that her son was stupid, we would have World War III, but the teacher has softened the blow, and the parent is feeling pretty good. When the teacher says the child is not working to his fullest capacity, the burden of responsibility is now exclusively on him. This is misplaced responsibility. The failure of the child also lies with the teacher and the parent. The following are questions I would like all parents to ask their child's teacher at some point during the school year:

✓ Where was my child at the beginning of the school year in each subject area?

✓ What skills/concepts has he/she acquired during this reporting period?

✓ Where is he/she in relation to your expectations at this point?

✓ What criteria did you use to establish your expectations for my child?

✓ How did you make your assessment of my child?

✓ What areas of strength have you identified in my child?

✓ What weaknesses have you identified in him/her?

✓ What are your plans for addressing these weaknesses?

✓ How can I assist in addressing the weaknesses?

✓ Is my child receiving any resource services outside the classroom? If so, please specify.

These are the kinds of questions that place the burden on the person who is being paid to educate your child. It is the job of the parents to assist and of the child to try, but it is the teacher's responsibility to provide a pedagogy, curriculum and environment that is conducive to learning.

Ideally speaking, the objective for those children who

are not in special education because of a physical impairment should be mainstreamed back into the regular classroom and expected to perform at a satisfactory level. Special education programs should not be designed to indefinitely warehouse children. I suggest to parents that they query the possibility of the child remaining in the mainstream classroom and of special education resources being brought into the classroom.

Regarding Ritalin, I believe the school system is becoming a larger drug dealer than the Mafia. There are presently four million children receiving Ritalin. Ritalin is a stimulant, an amphetamine. I've always thought it was a contradiction to prescribe an amphetamine for hyperactivity. Ritalin's side effects are loss of appetite, sleeping difficulties, and lethargy. It is my opinion that before Ritalin is given, a change in instructional pedagogy and curriculum should be implemented. I also encourage parents to visit the classroom, observe their child and make their own honest and informed assessment. If the school is unwilling to make any concessions, parents may have to identify an alternative public or private school which may present financial and/or residential hardships.

Of all the concerns in the letters that I receive, the issue of special education far exceeds all others.

Dear Dr. Kunjufu:

I have heard you say once that if a child fails a grade between kindergarten and third grade, there is a 70 percent chance that he will not graduate from high school.

I never forgot that statement, and it has me worried now. The school has indicated that they want to retain my child in kindergarten because they don't feel that he has mastered what a five-year-old child should have during this past school year. I believe my child is smart, but of course I am just a mother. The people with the degrees have a different answer, and they feel that my child would benefit from remaining in kindergarten an extra year. They also think that it will make him more mature.

I know that you don't know me and you don't know my child, but I am wondering, what should I do? I don't want children to call my child slow or dummy. I don't want him to wonder why he is not able to keep up with his friends in class. I don't know what that will do to his self-esteem. Please call me collect as soon as you can.

I wonder about parents who express concern on the last day of school when they find out their child has not been, e.g. promoted to the next grade. There must have been obvious warning signs during the first, second and third quarters of the school year. At my workshops, I have parents provide their child's grades based on homework, and test scores they have reviewed. When a child and his parents are expecting an A and the teacher gives the child a D or a C, there is missing information in the scenario that needs to be discovered. Parents who have monitored their child's progress throughout the year should not be surprised in any given quarter, and definitely not at year's end. I also have parents determine whether there was a disparity between the report card and national achievement test scores. If the child has done well in either one, then the parent has an important argument to use for promoting the child into the next grade.

After I collect this data, I quiz the parents: What kind of academic stimulation is being provided for children at home? Are there regular visits to the library? Is there any reading of stories to children or by children?

Next, I want parents to give me some idea of how many children were in the class and whether there were any other children that failed. Were there a disproportionate number of African American males retained?

I agree that retainment is necessary if mastery has not been achieved. Society has a right to expect that anyone in possession of a high school diploma can read, write, and compute at a certain agreed upon level. If schools don't enforce their standards, employers will lack confidence in graduates receiving promotions, diplomas and degrees. I am against social promotion, e.g., children can only fail once because the school does not want older children to remain in lower grades or because it is more expensive to educate children for several years in the same grade. This practice does not take into account what they do or don't do during the school year. Can you imagine how difficult it is for a classroom teacher to hold children accountable when they know that regardless of what they do, they have to be promoted?

I advise parents to consider their options. As soon as they see a problem, provide additional tutors at home. Increase study time. Deny privileges at home. What my teachers told me must hold true for us with our children today. They said they refused to allow me to fail. What they meant was that I was not allowed to fail my class and whatever it took to make sure I passed - extra time, energy, resources, home visits, field trips, speeches given by role models - they would provide it.

Lastly, I tell parents facing retainment of their child that they can appeal to the principal and the school board to have their child "condition" to the next grade. This puts the child on a 10-week trial period, during which time the child must demonstrate mastery of a subject(s) based upon clearly defined and mutually agreed upon criteria. This allows parents one more opportunity to circumvent the problem.

Dear Dr. Kunjufu:

I enjoyed hearing you speak a few months ago in my city. I don't know if you remember, but I mentioned to you after the presentation that I was having problems with my son. He seemed to fit your Fourth Grade Failure Syndrome to a "T." He seemed to be motivated and interested in school in K-3, but with each grade since then his interest has waned. He is now in seventh grade, and he's just completely lackadaisical as it relates to academics. Of course he loves his friends, rap, and sports. I do the very best I can as a single mother (who works nights) to monitor his whereabouts, but I'm afraid that at the pace that he is going he may get caught up in the wrong crowd and join a gang and drop out of school. I was wondering if you could write to him or give him a call, or possibly on your next visit to my city, stop by and visit. Just give me a call at your earliest convenience. My heart is heavy and I know you understand.

My first question in this type of situation is, Does the child have a positive male role model? He doesn't have to be the father. There are numerous homes, including mine, where the father is very literate and accomplished, but the children are not inspired to read and take academics as seriously as they should. Many parents tell me that I have said the same thing to their child as a role model that they've said as parents, but that it meant so much more coming from another person. I think it is very important that for children, especially African American boys, to be exposed to positive male role models.

Additionally, I encourage parents to have their child read *To Be Popular or Smart: the Black Peer Group.* Since peers are the number one influence on our children, every effort should be made to monitor peer pressure. Parents should know their children's friends and their parents. Parents should get phone numbers, invite their children's friends over, program the children's peer group with activities that reinforce your value system and have your children check back regularly when they are outside playing.

I also encourage parents to read *Maggie's American Dream* by James Comer and *Gifted Hands* by Ben Carson, and to watch *Up Against the Wall,* starring Marla Gibbs, and the *Mary Thomas story* about Mrs. Thomas raising former NBA Star Isaiah Thomas. These four strong Black women were able to raise their sons in poverty, squalor and mire because of their relationship with the Lord and their will power. I also recommend that they read *Family Life and School Achievement* by Reginald Clark, who discounts the role of money and the number of parents participation in quality interaction between parent and child as the key factors in raising healthy children.

Parents need to review not only the literature but also that in the school's curriculum for its accuracy and relevance to their children's lives. Many times I have sent literature to schools to rebut the fallacy that Columbus discovered America, Lincoln freed slaves and Egypt is in the Middle East.

Lastly, children are bored only when they are boring people. Parents should help their sons find engaging hobbies. They should try to find out what their sons' interests are and secure reading materials in that area. If a son likes rap, subscribe to a rap magazine or get biographies of famous rappers. Children can improve their reading skills while reading material they enjoy.

This last letter comes from the parents of an older youth.

Dear Dr. Kunjufu,

I hope this letter finds you and your family doing well. I've enjoyed reading your work and hearing you speak. I know this is an unfair question, but I'll ask it anyway. What do you do with a 19-year-old son who has graduated from high school, can't find a job and simply wants to lie around my house all day long and eat the food that I buy and is too lazy to even help me carry the food up the steps? I threw up my hands seven or eight years ago when he was 12, and said, I don't know what to do with him. I said that in a moment of frustration, but now that he is 19, I really don't know what to do with this boy. I have two younger children that I need to raise, and hopefully they won't end up like him. I'm tired. I have my own life to live. So what would you suggest? Just kick him out? The military? What can I do? Please write or call soon.

In responding to this type of letter, I tell parents about the opposite sex dynamics. Apparently, humans in Western countries are not as skilled at pushing their children out of the nest as in Eastern countries and in the animal kingdom. It is a greater challenge when the opposite gender is involved. Mothers seem to do a much better job of preparing their daughters to leave than their sons. Fathers seem to do a much better job with their sons than their daughters. We have a rule at our house: we will give you everything you *need* for the first 18 years of your life, and on your 18th birthday you must leave, preferably for college. Parents have a dilemma when their sons are not college material and have no immediate plans for the future. Who wants to spend $10,000 to $15,000 a year for a student who's not serious? It is mind boggling when you consider that children who receive money from parents may not do well, but when the money is cut off, and the students are forced to pay their own way through school, they seem to do much better.

Many of our youth believe that they have the option, though not preferable, of remaining in the parent's home. This allows them to play grownup while acting like children. Many youth, because of materialism, want to live in their parents' house but spend their money on Western trinkets instead of rent, utilities and food. This, in my opinion, can deceive children about reality. I wish there was an institution similar to a dormitory where parents could send unmotivated youth who want to be grownup but can't pay for it.

When the mother mentioned that her son was unemployed, I wondered how aggressively he has been looking for employment. Mothers need to put the fire under their sons and let them know that their stay cannot be indefinite. Obviously, if a person did not have a support system, he'd have to look for work day-by-day, if not hour-by-hour, and accept whatever was available. When children are allowed to be irresponsible, they often don't feel compelled to accept minimum wage jobs like washing dishes or commission sales.

The military option is more complex. There are many mothers who have used the military to teach their sons responsibility and have been successful. I am concerned, though, about how parents can say I don't know what to do with him after 18 years and expect the military to teach them discipline in two to three months. I could give you horror stories on the abuse and the disproportionate number of African American males who have received a dishonorable discharge, which can affect their employment opportunities for the rest of their lives. I could also mention studies illustrating that the military has been fairer to African American males than corporate America. Retired General Colin Powell showed us that there is no glass ceiling in the military in contrast to the Fortune 500. That does not mean that racism does not exist in the military. African American males are only six percent of the population, but they are one-third of the military. There remains a disproportionate percentage of African American males on the front-line and involved in combat duty. I am concerned with our sons being on the front-line especially in places like Haiti, Rwanda, Liberia and Nigeria. In a world based on White supremacy, African males from various countries don't need to kill each other to maintain the oppression of its people. I encourage mothers to attend the registration meetings with the military and monitor the application. If your son has expressed an interest in electronics, aviation or another technical field that is noncombative, every effort should be made to attain that reality.

I usually close my letters or conversations by imploring the mother to stay strong and give her son tough love. I remember my father telling me that if I ever got locked up he was not going to get me out. My mother said she would, but my father told her, "Don't even think about it." I knew he meant it, and even though I didn't like what he said, I am raising my sons by similar rules. For many parents, the problem is the lack of rules. For others, it's the ability to enforce them. If the consequence of breaking the rules is kicking the child out of the house, then you must be prepared to follow through. With the streets as dangerous as they are, mothers are reluctant to have their sons leave and become the victim of an act of violence that she will always think was her fault and could have been prevented. It's the choice between a rock and a hard place. If the rock is allowing my son to stay home and be irresponsible, and the hard place is taking the chance that my son will be a victim of an act of violence, I'm going to take the hard place because it is the only hope for teaching responsibility. If mothers allow their sons to stay with them irresponsibly, they may be physically alive but they are mentally, emotionally, financially and spiritually bankrupt and dead. When one mother said that her son eats up all the food in her house, yet was too lazy to help her carry the food, in my opinion death has already begun.

I wish mothers of sons could have a conference to benefit and derive strength from each other. Mothers are worrying about and suffering from similar problems, but they are responding individually without support. They are waiting in school offices by themselves. They are arguing with school clerks, teachers and principals by themselves. They are meeting with four professionals about their son's future by themselves. They are tackling lack of motivation, peer pressure, gangs and other vices by themselves.

In many cities mothers who have buried their sons due to wanton violence have organized themselves into various groups: Mothers Against Gangs, Mothers Against Violence, Mothers Against Crime. Most had not considered getting together until a tragedy happened to their sons. I commend them for coming together to try to prevent another child from being a victim.

I wish we could organize mothers before their sons' lives are snuffed out at an early age. Not only do we need these groups, but we need Mothers Against Ritalin, Mothers Against a Disproportionate Number of Black Boys Failing Kindergarten, Mothers Against Special Education, Mothers against Teachers That Give Our Boys Low Expectations and Mothers Against Gangster Rap.

The following chapter will explore the relationship between female teachers and Black boys.

Photo by Glen Norris

When a Black boy looks at a female teacher with a look of defiance, I call this "the showdown."

CHAPTER SIX

Female Teachers and Black Male Culture

Female teachers, especially White ones, are integral in the development of Black boys in America. Since the Brown vs. Topeka case of 1954, desegregation has more than ever brought Black boys into contact with White females. In light of this, it can be noted that 83 percent of all elementary teachers are females. Black children constitute 17 percent of all students but comprise 41 percent of all special education placements, primarily as Educable Mentally Retarded (EMR) and Behavioral Disorder (BD). Of the Black children placed in special education, almost 85 percent are boys. African American males lead the nation in suspensions.

These statistics raise numerous questions. Why are Black children disproportionately labeled EMR and BD? Why are Black boys labeled EMR and BD more than girls? Is there any relationship between female teachers and Black boys being placed in EMR and BD classes and/or suspended? What are the differences between Black and White female teachers in their impact on Black boys? Are there differences between male and female teachers as they relate to Black male children? Who's responsible for the plight of Black boys in school?

In American society, the victims are often blamed because they have the fewest resources to defend themselves. Black people are blamed for their plight yet are the only racial group that did not come to America voluntarily looking for a better life. Scholars, like Ryan in *Blame the Victim* and others, realize the blame may lie with the perpetrator. It is not my desire to blame either Black boys or female teachers. This would be just as useless as teachers blaming parents and parents blaming teachers while children suffer. My concern is based on the realistic profile that Black boys, in their nine years (K-8) of elementary school, may encounter a maximum of two male teachers - possibly none. And if male teachers are available, they will be in the upper grades, beyond the all-important fourth grade.

The educational future of our boys must be based on mutual understanding and respect. Instead, I feel that schools have placed the burden of blame on boys for their lack of achievement. Even the NCAA rule 48 places the major responsibility on the "athlete-student" to achieve a 2.0 grade point average and 16 or 800 on the ACT or SAT respectively. Often this is not achieved since elementary schools still operate with "social promotion," i.e., children are passed because of age rather than competency.

To evaluate the relationship of female teachers and Black male students, let's first look at female teachers. I believe that how women feel about themselves affects their pedagogy. How women feel about their father, boyfriend, husband - or the lack thereof - is also significant. Women who have been abused or raped, either in childhood or marriage, have serious issues to deal with. In the broad range between the traditional wife and the lesbian lies our female teaching corps. On the issues of sexism, contemporary literature like *For Colored Girls Only* and *The Color Purple* have an impact on teacher attitudes. Do you really believe that the way female teachers feel about themselves, men and sexism can be left at home and not enter the classroom? What structure exists for female teachers to unload these complicated feelings, or to objectively determine if they are affecting their male students? What college education department equips female students to isolate these variables for consideration?

For White women it becomes more complex, because their Black students may be the first Black males with whom they have ever had direct contact. This amazes me. How can you teach a child who you do not know or understand?

Unfortunately, in an insecure world, most people equate differences with deficiencies. Black people are different from Whites, and insecure Whites will use this as evidence of White superiority. My position is that Black boys are different from White boys and Black and White girls, but not better or worse. All teachers must develop strategies to maximize African American boys' potential.

Now let's look at African American culture, male culture and their synthesis, Black male culture. It is a sad commentary, but many Blacks do not feel they have a culture. I have not only been told that by Black adults but I have also witnessed it in the actions of children. A friend of mine shared with me that a teacher of an international class of children requested that they bring an ethnic dish and wear their cultural dress. The Chinese, Mexican and German students knew what to bring and wear, but the two Black students brought hamburgers and french fries and wore blue jeans and t-shirts. I could not fault the students because they only expressed the lack of cultural awareness of their parents. W. E .B. Du Bois, in the *Souls of Black Folks*, eloquently describes the "double consciousness and warring souls" - one African, the other American - and the difficulty of trying to be African (Black) in White America or being American (White) in the Black community. Many Blacks give up trying to please either soul and they become very individualistic. Their motto is, "I'm just trying to be me."

I feel compelled to describe my culture. Had it not been for chattel and mental slavery, I would be dressing my son in a dashiki and my daughter in a buba with her hair wrapped in a gele or profiling cornrows, not French braids or the Bo Derek look. For "International Festival Day," they would have brought mangoes, avocados, plantains, watermelons, millet, okra, black-eyed peas and curried chicken. Their notebooks would have pyramid designs and hieroglyphics on them, and they would know that Egypt is in Africa, not the Middle East, and that Egyptians, not Greeks and Romans, built the first civilization. The red, black and green flag would be saluted daily in their classroom. When other children greeted them in their native language, my children would say, "habari gani," which means, "What's the news?" in Swahili. Lastly, I would require that the next "International Festival" not be held on January 15, in February, on May 19, June 19, August 17, or December 26 through January 1 (the holy days honoring Dr. King, Black History Month, Malcolm X, Juneteenth, Marcus Garvey and Kwanzaa, respectively) because my children would not be there.

Not all Blacks may agree with me on my idea of an empowering African American culture, so let's look at what kind of culture we do have.

Language-	Black English, rappin,' slang, oral rather than written
Music-	Soul, blues, jazz, gospel, rap
Food-	Soul food, spicy, plentiful
Dress-	Bright colors, flashy design
Religion-	Minister-congregation-call chant response, high percentage of community involvement
Learning style-	Right brain, relational, people oriented

I often hear terms like "culturally disadvantaged," "culturally deprived," "dominant culture" and "subculture." These are arrogant terms. Everyone has a culture, including a people with two warring souls. Culture is lifestyle; it represents the what and how of everything you do.

We cannot afford to have teachers placing negative value judgments on Black culture. When a five-year-old Black child enters kindergarten speaking the language of his or her environment, which may happen to be Black English, this child's self-esteem should not have to withstand teacher condemnation. I am not in favor of our children speaking Black English, but the self-esteem of the child should not be harmed when the transfer is made from Black to Standard English. White female teachers interacting with Black students for the first time need to understand and appreciate this new culture - Black English, rappin, slang, soul, blues, jazz, rhythm, Black dress, food, Black standards of beauty, and holistic learning styles. How can you teach a child you do not understand or respect? Black, Hispanic and White children are culturally different, but not culturally disadvantaged, unless the definer is culturally arrogant.

Let's now look at some of the traits of African American male culture:

Ego-	Larger and more sensitive than that of most girls
Macho-	Prefers handling problems physically rather than emotionally
Athletic-	Values athletics more than academic pursuits
Noncommunicative-	Less emotional, accent on being "cool"
Risk-	Peer group uses risk as their rite of passage

Teachers who have a healthy respect for Black male culture developed their appreciation in childhood. For those teachers who were not similarly blessed, college education departments should offer courses on understanding male culture. I am not suggesting that a course is not also needed for female culture, but I am advocating that in this country where a disproportionate number of females are teaching a large number of boys who are not reaching academic standards, this course is essential. The issue of male culture transcends race: White and Hispanic boys are also known for their ego, aggression, athletic orientation, non-communication, and risk taking.

The rate of progress of the members of these three groups is directly influenced by institutional racism and teachers' ability to understand these cultures. Hispanic males have the highest dropout rate, which is attributed to the language barrier and the strict gender role expectation of being the family's provider regardless of age. Black males disproportionately lead in special education placements, suspensions, and athletic scholarships (The latter will be curtailed with NCAA rules 48, 42, 16, and 14.) White males also suffer from a female-run classroom, but when placed in special education rather than EMR, they are usually classified learning disabled (LD), where the curriculum and teacher's expectations remains challenging. White males need only to finish high school to exceed the income levels of all other groups with college degrees. My concern remains for Black and Hispanic males who are not as fortunate. That's why Lerone Bennett, executive editor of *Ebony Magazine* and author says, "The question of education for Black people in America is a question of life and death. It is a political question, a question of power. Struggle is a form of education, perhaps the highest form."[1]

Let's now combine the Black culture of language, music, food, dress, religion and learning style with male culture, which consists of ego, aggression, athletics, noncommunication, and risk taking. The synthesis should provide a reasonable view of Black male culture. Black male culture encompasses all e.g., the characteristics of male culture and Black culture with one important exception - religion. Large numbers of Black boys think the church is for women and sissies.

Expressions of this synthesis are rap music or the lines men give women, "dozens" (signifyin'), "the walk" (the leaning of the head with a cap and a tremendous regard for the peer group. (Other classroom characteristics will be provided in chapter eight on curriculum.) Female teachers must understand that Black boys value their peers, their walk, rap and signifyin' more than anything else. Teachers are not going to sway these boys to their way of thinking with a condemnation of things the boys value. Many female teachers are not aware of the value system Black boys hold dear. College education departments don't teach the importance of these things. Not only that, there are many of us who grew up in the culture but express disdain and condescension for it. Please do not think that condemnation will sap a boy's desire to value his culture expressions. Condemnation may instead cause him to defend these expressions.

I am not condoning the dozens, or any other negative facet of Black male culture, but if we want to save Black boys, we must transfer their cultural strengths into the classroom experience. This chapter is designed to familiarize teachers with Black male culture. Chapter eight will attempt to show how these cultural patterns can be integrated into the curriculum to maximize student achievement. A group acceptance will take this into consideration when making public admonishments. For example, there is one characteristic that is the most misunderstood and causes Black boys to be suspended or placed in EMR and BD classes. It's the "dozens."

The dozens is an activity primarily performed by males, in which usually two opponents dual verbally. They make derogatory comments about each other and each other's family members, usually the mother. The performance of each player is appreciated and judged by the group who urges them on. This is called a manhood rite because it serves an important function. The boy must master several important competencies in order to be a good player. First of all, he must control his emotions. Here in the presence of his friends, terribly derogatory statements are made about his mother, who is dear to him. He must suppress his emotional reaction to what has been said so that he can think quickly and counter with an even more clever slur upon his opponent's mother. Unfortunately, when Black male children volley verbally in an aggressive, threatening manner,

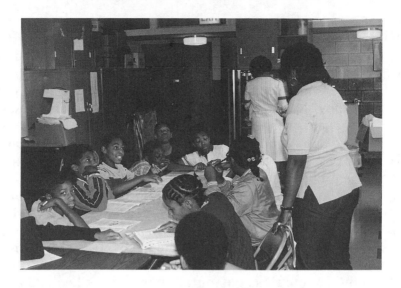

When Black male children volley verbally in an aggressive manner, some teachers don't understand.

---

some teacher's misunderstand and interpret their behavior as fighting, when actually they were signifyin' to relieve tension and *avoid* a fight. Large numbers of Black males are labeled as having disciplinary problems or being EMR, and are often suspended because of the dozens or signifyin.' People who do not understand Black culture take words of this rite literally. When Black parents tell their children, "I'm going to knock you into the middle of next week," the phrase needs to be tempered with a Black cultural perspective.

An important component of both Black culture and Black male culture is the oral tradition. Principals express disappointment in men when only a few parents attend the PTA meeting, although hundreds of notices were sent out. My experience has been that institutions like Head Start, with a parent coordinator staff and a principal who personally solicits PTA attendees, receive a far greater response. For Black boys, the ability to rap, e.g., rhyme, to influence a girlfriend, mother, and, if possible, the teacher, is valued because they come from a strong oral tradition. In chapter eight, I will discuss how the walk, the tilted head and the hat affect the learning process.

Ten-year-old Renee has light skin, "good" hair, "keen" features, and "pretty" eyes. She wears nice lace dresses with a ribbon in her hair daily. She is slightly shy, but has a radiant smile that she flashes when complimented.

Willie is also ten, but is big for his age. He has dark skin, short "nappy" hair, and "broad" features. Willie wears the same jeans to school everyday for one week, but only wears the shirt twice. He talks loudly and shows off in front of his friends. His arms are often crossed defiantly. Are your expectations the same for both students? What do you feel when a 10-year-old Black boy folds his arms and looks you directly in the eye?

When a Black boy looks at the female teacher with a look of defiance, I call this the "showdown" between female teachers and Black boys. If the dozens did not exclude him from the mainstream, in most instances the showdown would. Black boys could avoid this confrontation if they looked and acted like Renee. Black males unfortunately are not always interested in being cooperative, quiet and dainty. Female teachers could avoid this exhibition if they would come out of themselves and appreciate Willie for what he represents. As we have asked before, Why are we unable to maintain boys' enthusiasm and achievement levels with each passing year? There are numerous reasons for this decline: less nurturance and physical activity; less student questions and parental involvement; greater influence by the peer group; more classroom competition; more left-brain, analytical and task-oriented learning; and fewer male teachers.

As boys grow tall, teachers are less able to use their prior advantage of size to discipline them.

The showdown will not always match strength against strength. Some female teachers are *afraid* of Black boys. I do not believe you can teach a child while afraid. This may be the reason why only 45 percent of all secondary teachers are women. Male teachers can be found in high schools, and possibly in upper elementary grades. The problem is that we are losing large numbers of Black boys before they reach grades eight through twelve. (I have also observed a very strong, effective teaching cadre in alternative schools, GED and adult education.) Principals continue to tell me that they must place their stronger teachers in the upper grades. This is a Band-Aid approach. How effective is this strategy when we are losing students before they encounter these "relief teachers"?

When a Black boy looks at the female teacher with a look of defiance, many factors are at stake. How do female teachers feel about themselves? How do they feel about men? Where are they on the continuum between "traditional" wife and "lesbian?" What has their exposure been to Black culture? Do they understand that our society is patriarchal? When they see Willie, do they see a future Jesse Jackson or a drug addict?

What is going on inside the Black boy at the showdown? Is he trying to show off in front of his friends? Is this one of the risks required for the rites of passage? Has he learned that discipline is associated with physical force, e.g., the belt, and does he feel confident now that he is bigger and his strength and size are in his favor? Does he really want to be taught, loved, understood and given some direction? Is he challenging the adult to e.g., determine if there is anyone capable of fulfilling his needs?

When the showdown begins, these are some of the potential outcomes:

(1) The female teacher, out of emotional control, hollers at the child. The class laughs. Willie sits down slowly causing further disruption. The class, Willie and probably the teacher know Willie won this battle.

(2) The female teacher responds inconsistently to Willie's behavior. He wins because she has never reproved his negative behavior in the past. If her response is unassertive, he also wins.

(3) The female teacher sends Willie downstairs to the principal's office. Probable actions include suspension, EMR placement and eventual expulsion. Willie wins against the female teacher because she was incapable of handling the situation herself. He may still lose to the principal or special education teacher.

(4) The female teacher sends Willie to the corner or outside the classroom door. This showdown is a draw; the battle has been delayed indefinitely.

(5) The female teacher assertively and consistently tells Willie to go to his seat and he complies. The female teacher wins all encounters.

The showdown is a battle of physical, emotional and intellectual strength, and adults cannot win without leverage. Many homes use the belt as the leverage. A major problem for schools occurs when children only respect physical punishment, not assertive communication, behavior modification and denial of privileges. Coaches are effective because they use uniforms, letters, game participation, trophies, scholarships and potential stardom as leverage. Teachers can possibly use grades, but this is ineffective if not reinforced in the home and if the students do not see the effect of good grades on their future place in society. The only other leverage a teacher (Black, White, male or female) has is when you exclude the belt, NBA, grades and jobs is the best combination of love, cultural understanding and mutual respect.

Some boys have decided to become the class clown not only to receive attention, but to camouflage their academic deficiencies. Their behavior includes the following:

- ❖ Ignoring their teachers;

- ❖ Carrying on non-academic discussions;

- ❖ Listening to music on headphones;

- ❖ Reading magazines;

- ❖ Cracking jokes;

- ❖ Making fun of other students;

- ❖ Throwing paper and other items;

- ❖ Playing hand held video and phone games;

- ❖ Attempting to cheat on exams;

- ❖ Sleeping

Experienced teachers who know their boys want to be suspended refuse. In addition, they have challenged their boys to entertain their students and many boys have declined or performed poorly.

The following chapter will explore providing a congruent pedagogy and curriculum for African American males.

CHAPTER SEVEN

A Relevant Curriculum and Pedagogy for Black Boys

I keep asking myself, "What kind of curriculum and pedagogy can we develop to maximize Black boys' potential?" Most formal workshops have not uncovered the answer to this research question because of institutional resistance to altering curriculae or teaching styles for the purpose of meeting the needs of Black children, specifically boys. I optimistically believe that most teachers would like to reach Black boys rather than place them in special education or on suspension, so I developed a workshop where participants can share ideas and successful lesson plans.

Unfortunately, there are teachers who teach with the attitude, "I got mine and you've got yours to get." Many teachers teach the way they were taught as children. They ask, "Why should I have to change the way I teach for Black boys?" In the Effective Schools Project, Ron Edmonds noted that in schools with low achievement, the most negative room in the school is the teachers' cafeteria. The room is filled with condescending negative comments about the futility of teaching "these children." Effective schools have a positive learning climate that does not allow this attitude to permeate its facility.[1]

Piaget says, "Instructors teach their subjects, but teachers understand how children learn." This idea helps us further understand the fourth-grade syndrome. As children move into the upper grades and high school, less concern is allocated to the student, and more attention is given to the subject matter. High school teachers will quickly inform you, "I am a geometry teacher" — not a teacher of children. Who cares that the student may be lacking in self-esteem, motivation or reading comprehension skills?

I open all my teacher workshops declaring "You cannot teach a child you do not love. You cannot teach a child you do not respect. You cannot teach a child you do not understand. You cannot teach a child you fear. You cannot teach a child before discarding your political baggage, e.g., sexism and racism." (How many teachers do you know that have the ability to keep their past experiences about racism and sexism outside the classroom door?) You cannot teach a child without bonding with him first. To bond, you must have love, respect and understanding.

When you teach Black boys, what do you see? A future engineer, doctor, accountant? Or do you see a drug dealer? Whatever you see will be what you produce. Do you have the same expectations for Black boys as cooperative girls? Research has shown that expectations are a major factor in student achievement. The problem is that often within the same classroom, teachers have different levels of expectation. The Teacher Expectations Student Achievement (TESA) model is an excellent tool to evaluate consistency. The model is divided into three separate categories for observation:

Response Opportunities	Feedback	Personal Regard
1) Equitable distribution	1) Affirm or correct student's performance	1) Proximity
2) Individual helping	2) Praise	2) Courtesy
3) Delving	3) Listening	3) Personal interests
4) Higher-level questioning	4) Accepting feelings	4) Touching

Can you honestly say that in each category and to the fourth degree you provide each child with the same level of expectations? Studies show that teachers give girls 3.2 seconds to respond to a question versus 2.7 for boys. The gap widens for Black girls and boys and becomes progressively wider over the school year.[2]

The critical question remains: What kind of curriculum and pedagogy can we develop to maximize Black boys' potential? I believe this question has been answered in numerous articles by A. W. Boykin, Henry Morgan and Na'im Akbar. Janice Hale,

Paulo Friere, James Banks and William Glasser have also contributed important information to this research. My favorite piece on this subject was written by Asa Hilliard of the Council of Independent Black Institutions (CIBI) and the Cultural Linguistic Approach (CLA). Listed below are a few salient salient ideas Hilliard offers:

The School

How it is Generally (analytical)	How it Could Be (relational)
Rules	Freedom
Standardization	Variation
Conformity	Creativity
Memory for specific facts	Memory for essence
Regularity	Novelty
Rigid order	Flexibility
"Normality"	Uniqueness
Differences equal deficiency	Sameness equals oppression
Preconceive	Improvise
Precision	Approximate
Logical	Psychological
Automistic	Global
Egocentric	Sociocentric
Convergent	Divergent
Controlled	Expressive
Meanings are universal.	Meanings are contextual.
Direct	Indirect
Cognitive	Affective
Linear	Patterned
Mechanical	Humanistic
Unison	Individual in group
Hierarchical	Democratic
Isolation	Integration
Deductive	Inductive
Scheduled	Targets of opportunity
Thing-focused	People-focused
Constant	Evolving
Sign-oriented	Meaning oriented
Duty	Loyalty[3]

Many psychologists connect this model to the split-brain theory. The brain is divided into two apparently symmetrical parts. The left side of the brain is analytical, divides things into sections, and specializes in the functions of math and science. The right hemisphere is holistic and relational and appreciates music, art, dance and sports. Returning to Piaget's comment about instructors and teachers, do we ignore the strength of Black children who process information on the right side of the brain? One factor of the fourth-grade failure syndrome is that with each grade level a more left-brain curriculum is implemented. A most graphic illustration of this is the large number of college graduates who draw on a primary level. The curriculum of most schools ignores most forms of learning other than the written word.

I offer five forms of instruction: written, oral, pictures, artifacts and fine arts.

The last four emphasize the right side of the brain. I am not suggesting that we should exclude the left hemisphere or analytical learning; that would be just as harmful as the present situation which excludes right-brain, relational learning. I'm advocating all five forms of instruction to help more children to grasp concepts. The following examples are offered:

(1) Two students are learning to dance, one with a left-brain analytical approach, the other with a right-brain relational approach. The first child goes to a dance studio and follows the floor chart until he succeeds. The second student goes to a disco, observes for a period of time, then gets on the dance floor and does his/her "own thing." Which approach is correct?

(2) The teacher announces she will give 100 points in extra credit for additional reading, 75 points for an oral presentation, and 10 points for an illustration. Is this evaluation fair to all learners?

(3) Teachers can assign students to:

  (a) Read and write the definitions.
  (b) Read the definition and trace the picture.
  (c) Read the definition and create your own image.

  Which exercise encompasses both analytical and relational learning?

(4) Children know that 6 x 3 = 18, but in a word problem they don't know when to use multiplication.

Example number four has several pedagogical and cognitive points that require illumination. The analytical learner who breaks an operation into parts is more comfortable separating a skill from its use. The relational learner needs to be given the objective before the skill is taught. An increasing number of students, including analytical thinkers, are lacking motivation because they don't see the relevance of the lesson. It concerns me that Black boys are labeled slow learners in the classroom and yet on the streets and in the military, they understand math and science applications very well.

How can a brother fail Math in school and yet, without pencil, paper or calculator, tell each one of his friends what he will pay for a bottle of Wild Irish Rose? Is it because the street curriculum is real and one mistake could be costly or deadly? Did the motivation to learn come before or after the skill? Military training is another excellent example of blending theory with practice, analytical with relational.

The military provides an overview of its objectives, followed by theoretical readings, and finally demonstrations on the actual equipment. Again, many Black boys that were placed in EMR and on suspension do very well in the military. (I am not overlooking institutional racism evident from the disproportionately high number of Black men on the front line as compared to behind the line where technicians and officers fulfill their imperialistic objectives.) A sound educational plan shows the need first and encourages questions.

Another component of the fourth-grade failure syndrome is the inverse relationship between age and questions. What is it about our pedagogy that produces unmotivated students who sit for long periods of time without asking questions? A comprehensive multicultural pedagogy uses a variety of lesson plans and evaluation instruments. The military not only teaches its students through reading, films and objects but also evaluates learning in written and oral tests and in field demonstrations.

The Cultural Linguistic Approach (a university curriculum research firm) based its educational curriculum in social studies, mathematics, science and language arts called USISPU:

U - Unstructured Elicitation
S - Structured Elicitation
I - Interim
S - Structured Elicitation
P - Practice
U - Unstructured Elicitation

A sample lesson plan

Concept: All people are alike and different in many ways.
Performance: The child will be able to identify people who are similar to him in the dimensions of race, sex and age.

Materials: Pictures — Black ABC's
           Filmstrips — *Getting to Know Me*
           Books — *Colors Around Me*

Procedure: Motivation — Teacher shows the class various pictures of Black children.

U- Tell me everything you can about this picture. (The objective is to use Black children's oral strength and cultural heritage to stimulate further cognition.)

S- Tell me what color skin this child has.
Tell me what color the child's eyes are.
Tell me something about the child's hair.

I- Class, these are pictures of Black children. Why do we call them Black children? How many of us think these children look like you?

There are lots of skin colors that little Black children have.

Have them draw a picture of themselves.

S- Tell me what color skin this child has.
Tell me what color his eyes are.
Tell me something about this child's hair.

P- My name is _____

I am _____ years old.

My eyes are _____.

My hair is _____.

I belong to the _____ race.

I am a _____ (boy/girl).

U- Tell me everything you can about this picture.[4]

This sample lesson plan would benefit Black children and all other children who have a relational orientation. In my workshops I often ask female teachers, "What are some of the differences between boys and girls in the classroom?" If we accept Piaget's contention about instructors and teachers, we must determine commonly observed male classroom characteristics in contrast to female characteristics, and then create a curriculum that will compliment it. The following list reflects brainstorming sessions I have had with teachers from across the country.

Male Classroom Characteristics

Aggressive

Athletic

Shorter attention span

Slower maturation rate

Less cooperative

Larger in size

Influenced more by peer group

Greater interest in math than reading

Gross motor skills greater than fine motor skills

Interested in fine arts

Not as neat

Louder

Prefer hats

Distinct walk

Larger and more sensitive ego

Signifying/dozens/rapping

I again want to return to the research question: What kind of curriculum and pedagogy can we develop to maximize Black boys' potential? Please review the male classroom characteristics. What curriculum changes or teaching styles should be altered within the context of these factors? I would like to isolate (1) shorter attention span, (2) greater influence of peer-group, (3) greater interest in math than in reading, (4) more advanced in gross versus fine motor skills, (5) keen interest in fine arts, (6) larger and more sensitive ego and (7) playing the dozens.

(1) Short attention span

Larger numbers of Black boys are put in special education because they are "hyperactive." This word is filled with value judgments and complexities. *Hyper* has to be based on a norm, which in America is White. Psychologists such as Garber, Boykin, and Wilson document the higher vibrancy, capital and verve that Black children bring into this world, which are reinforced in a highly stimulating home and street environment.

Black children with greater verve are often bored with *Mr. Rogers* and love *Sesame Street*. Unfortunately, the classroom is paced like *Mr. Rogers*. Black children, especially Black boys, may not be hyperactive but alternatively perhaps the curriculum is too slow. I suggest that the pace of classes be set fairly for everyone, not just whites or females who may be comfortable with *Mr. Rogers'* pace. I suggest that lectures, readings and individual tasks be shortened, and that more group projects and movement to hands-on learning centers be incorporated. If geometry, history, physics and English teachers can't provide hands-on experiences like the military, then the lack of motivation, best expressed by poor grades, boredom and cheating, will continue. I would also suggest that Black parents reduce their children's sugar in-take and television viewing and lead meditation exercises.

(2) The peer group

A teacher who is sensitive and respectful of the culture will not embarrass a child in front of the highly valued peer group. In one of my classes I asked the students, "How do you stay cool with your friends?" Almost all of them said by breaking the rules and by getting poor grades. I also asked them about things they wanted to improve — career goals, etc. — and they all invariably had high ambitions and wanted to do well. How can they individually want to do right, but collectively want to do wrong? How can a child act one way by himself and be totally different in front of his friends? (That reminds me of the cowardly KKK member who hides behind sheets and the street gang member who hides behind his identifiers. They are both afraid of one-on-one confrontations, but thrive on participating in gang beatings.)

I see the peer group as one of my competitors, but I also respect its influence. Unless children have strong self-esteem as well as peer esteem we will not be able to strip the peer group of its power. The best way to approach the peer group is through reprogramming, not elimination. The session titled Unity/Criticism/Unity (U/C/U), which I describe in detail in my book *Developing Positive Self-Images and Discipline in Black Children* attempts, with adult direction, to let the peer group mediate conflict. We have to find ways to reprogram the male peer group to believe that being smart is being cool.

(3) Interest in math than in reading

In a left-brain oriented curriculum, subjects are taught in isolation from each other. Reading and writing, reading and science, reading and math, art and math, etc., are taught separately. A more interdisciplinary approach is called for. There needs to be an avalanche of word problems infused into the math curriculum. Please remember, because of Black children's oral orientation, they should be encouraged to explain their operations at the board.

Problems in reading are a result of the movement in recent years away from phonics, the increase in television viewing and the lack of relevant books for Black children in the classroom. Reading comes before skill applications, and a relevant curriculum would provide Black children books that describe their cultural experiences.

(4) Advanced in gross motor skills

Large numbers of Black boys enter the primary division behind girls in fine motor functions. Homes that supply boys exclusively with trucks and balls do not help their sons on school projects that accentuate pencils, crayons and scissors. Teachers should not only be aware of the double standards at home but should give boys more time on fine motor functions

101

without valuing one over the other. Black boys simply have had less exposure to toys or other instruments that might encourage fine motor skills. The statement that boys maturation rate is slow is too simplistic and does not account for the nature/nurture relationship. Please understand that these same clumsy boys could become excellent brain surgeons. Learning centers need to build both skills, with teachers evaluating boys and girls equally. Fill your classroom with science projects, animals and plants.

(5) Keen interest in fine arts

I suggest that every concept presented in the classroom should include readings, oral presentations, pictures, artifacts and *fine arts*. Black boys often express their cognition and sensitivity through art. Black boys often learn a speech or story better through music than a book. A person who chooses to teach Black children without music or art is an instructor, not a teacher. Fine arts and the oral tradition are two cornerstones of Black culture. Thus, an excellent lesson plan might culminate every unit with a play. Does it really matter if students express their understanding on paper, orally, with a portrait, an object or dramatically?

(6) Large and sensitive egos

In a patriarchal society controlled by White men and with very few Black male role models available, Black boys don't know how to express their male ego. Creative teachers not only must teach boys to differentiate between battles and wars but they also must find ways for boys' leadership abilities to be expressed. This will not happen with female teachers who bring their political baggage into the classroom. Suggestions include:

    (a) Encourage boys to be the Master of Ceremonies in assemblies.

    (b) Encourage boys to be captains of learning centers and academic teams.

    (c) Designate the most aggressive boys as classroom monitors.

    (d) Encourage boys to read aloud and go to the board.

(7) **Playing the dozens, signifying and rapping**

In chapter 7 the dozens were explained. In this section we will look at how this skill can be transferred into the classroom. When I see a Black boy demonstrate the ability to play the dozens or signify, I see a person who:

(a) has quick thinking skills.
(b) understands rhyme.
(c) is expanding his vocabulary.
(d) has public speaking potential.

This can be used in debate, language arts, poetry, spelling bees, drama, etc. I would stop every game of the dozens and turn it into:

(a) a spelling bee.
(b) a debate, and I choose the topic.
(c) a word game where I say a word and we see how many other rhyming words can be given. The winner is the one who lasts the longest.
(d) a dramatic presentation.
(e) a game called "Nightline" where I let them discuss issues in an investigative style.

I repeat, you cannot teach a child that you do not understand or with whom you have not bonded. I would not accept the dozens in my classroom, but I *understand it*. And I let the boys know how good they are and that *these skills* can be transferred into other areas. As a teacher who understands the culture of the students that I teach, I use its strengths, not mine, to answer the question, "What kind of curriculum and pedagogy can we develop to maximize Black boys' potential?"

The next chapter will illustrate adolescence and the African American male's quest for a high school diploma.

Adolescence will reflect how well we've done our job.

CHAPTER EIGHT

Adolescence, Diploma and Entropy

"I don't even recognize my son. Does he love me? I think he shows me. I'm not going to ever have children again. Something happens to them when they become thirteen. They must all take some pill or drug or go to another planet called teenageville. When he was in second grade he used to run home from school and tell me about his spelling grades. I used to love it when he called me mama. He could always get whatever he wanted from me when he said, 'Mama, I love you.' But last night, I asked him where he was going and when he would be coming back. He looked at me, then he looked through me, and for a moment, I was afraid of him. It was as if my 17-year-old son had never come out of me."

These are just some of the comments from parents, especially mothers, who are trying to figure out how they are going to get through this next development hurdle. Adolescence is a very trying period, especially for sons and their mothers. It's also a challenging time for larger communities. We adults have relinquished control of our communities to teenage males, ages 13 to 18. Young, angry male predators have made us all, women, elders, even men, afraid to walk our own streets at night. This age group has forced schools to consider whether or not they should have guards or metal detectors at every door. Teachers are now more concerned about safety than education, and students are often afraid to walk to school.

This sad state of affairs brings us to the mother-son relationship. Many parents want a buddy-to-buddy relationship with their children, to be on a first-name basis, to hang out. Boys often treat their mothers like girlfriends or some other girl to try a line out on. Many boys learn how to manipulate their mothers out of doing chores, homework and other responsibilities. For example, they tell me they have eight times to empty the garbage: seven times to listen to their mothers' nagging, and one time to do it when she becomes very assertive and clear.

In chapter five I wrote about some mothers who *raise* their daughters and *love* their sons. They teach their daughters to study, cook and sew. They make them attend church and they expose them to other educational and cultural programs. These activities are optional for their sons. One of the major difficulties that youth workers struggle with is the lack of support they receive from parents with older boys. During earlier developmental stages, parents are more supportive in mandating their children's attendance in constructive programs. For some reason, parents who become buddies with their older sons allow them to decide whether they should go to church, attend an extra tutorial session or participate in extracurricular activities.

In *To Be Popular or Smart: The Black Peer Group*, I suggested the need for parents to organize a parental support group so that the mothers can openly discuss their teenage children, primarily their boys. Many parents are responding to difficult situations individually and feel isolated from the larger community. Just knowing that you're not alone is consoling. I'm optimistic that not only can we provide a bond for each other but solutions as well.

This period of adolescence is when the larger society begins to acknowledge the male shortage. It has been brought to my attention by the staff members of one high school that the junior and senior proms are not always attended by both males and females and that larger numbers of females now go unescorted to the prom. I was stunned when I heard this. I just couldn't comprehend that girls would go to the prom without a date. Apparently the girls chose to attend because the alternative would be to miss a very memorable experience in their lives. I was aware that girls often don't go to the prom with someone from their own class, but the fact that they are unable to find a male in the immediate vicinity illustrates the magnitude of this problem.

In large urban areas, the dropout rate hovers near 50 percent, and in a few cities the percentage is greater. The reasons for the high dropout rate are boredom, lack of finances, lack of rewarding experiences in school, lack of positive adult reinforcement and lack of safety. Our boys are extremely bored with the irrelevant curriculum presented in conjunction with low teacher expectations.

Schools are giving children a 1910 curriculum in the 21st century. I spoke to a group of teachers in New York who insisted that Black boys were not good in math. One of them had to admit, however, that they were great at working with metrics. She wondered why. When Black boys hear terms like kilos and grams, their interest peaks because they finally see the relevance of the classroom to the streets.

I enjoy speaking to all groups — students, parents and teachers — but the group that gives me the greatest satisfaction is adolescent boys. Schools often tell me they are undisciplined, disrespectful and have short attention spans. So educators are amazed to see their boys respond so well to my presentations. I tell them that my success at bonding with these students is due to my relationship with God; I tell them the truth, and they know it comes from their brother who loves them. What I like about our youth is that they're honest. They will tell you exactly how they feel. When they hear the truth from someone who cares about them, they are disciplined and respectful.

We have to improve our curriculum by making it multicultural, Africentric and relevant. It is surprising how a simple change in the curriculum can reduce the dropout rate and improve attendance. You cannot separate the curriculum from the disseminator; they are part of the same package. There are three kinds of adults in our classrooms: instructors, teachers and coaches. Instructors specialize in dispensing information. Many of them will tell you they teach geometry, physics or english. Instructors don't teach *children*, they teach their *subjects*. Instructors are people that aspire to be college professors. Teachers on the other hand, understand their subjects and can accommodate a variety of learning styles. Coaches have the ability to combine subject matter and learning styles with identity and self-esteem.

Unfortunately, from the fourth grade on we have too many instructors teaching our youth. Most African American boys require coaches that understand content, learning styles and self-esteem. We need coaches, not instructors, to teach our students.

It has been rewarding visiting high schools where many of my friends are coaches. They almost single-handedly decreased the dropout rate because of the bond that they share with the students. The students do not want to disappoint the coach. One committed coach in the lives of our children can make the difference.

My concern is that coaches burn out faster than instructors. Coaches give more and are in the minority. Instructors, who are the majority, give less and are often found in the teacher's lounge condemning our youth; they seldom burn out. We need strong administrators who will find creative ways to keep our coaches inspired and hold instructors accountable.

The high dropout rate is also a result of the disproportionate number of Black males that are suspended. African American males are eight percent of public school students nationwide but constitute 37 percent of the suspensions. Numerous studies indicate that African Americans are suspended for infractions, while other students receive warnings for the same violations. African American males that have been suspended for many days risk not matriculating due to unfulfilled attendance requirements.

My travels have taken me to school districts where a major difference exists in the suspension rates between high schools that have similar demographics. Why is it that one high school with an effective administrator, a committed staff and clearly stated guidelines, can have a much lower suspension rate than another school? We can't afford to lose African American boys to ineffective schools or have them fail due to suspension. For these reasons, I'm also in favor of in-house suspension. In this way, the violation will be served, but attendance will be maintained. My staff at African American Images has designed the Malcolm X room to provide an educational and cultural experience for infractions. Trained staff provide resource materials and a program similar to Scared Straight. The Autobiography of Malcolm X is required reading for staff and students. My only hesitancy is that students may choose to be suspended to take advantage of this cultural experience.

It was going to be a big day in the Taylor house, for today, their son Marlon was graduating from high school. It was nearing 7 p.m. and the limousine was waiting outside for the Taylor clan. It had been a very special year for Marlon. He had attended the senior prom in the same limousine. It was a beautiful white Lincoln stretch with large whitewall tires, a TV, VCR, CD player and telephone. The Taylor family was very proud of their son. He had achieved what his parents had been unable to achieve because of circumstances beyond their control. Family members from around the state had traveled to participate in this very special occasion. Some of the family went straight to school, but others came to the house for pregraduation pictures with ulterior hopes of riding in the limousine. Marlon was upstairs putting on his white suit jacket (that coincidentally matched the limousine) and combing his hair for the twenty-seventh time. Everything seemed to be in place. The whole family looked forward to the glorious occasion just one hour away.

When Marlon walked down the stairs, you would have thought that someone was announcing Mandela from South Africa or Clinton from the United States. That is exactly how Marlon felt, and that is how the Taylor family received him. Thank God they rented a stretch limousine because there were eleven people that rode in it from the Taylor house to Frederick Douglass High School. The family had much to be proud of. Four years ago, there had been 300 entering freshman students, 150 male and 150 female. Four years later, there were only 200 students graduating, 125 females and 75 males, and Marlon Taylor was one of them.

When they arrived at the high school, they took more pictures. The Taylor family was not alone in laying out the red carpet for their children; this was a big occasion for most Black families in this city. After an additional fifteen minutes of picture taking, the Taylor family entered the auditorium and tried to get seats close to the front. Marlon went into the room with his graduating class. The principal, Mrs. Roberts, the assistant principal, Mr. Johnson and the teachers were assisting students with their caps and gowns. Marlon was teasing some of the sisters and playing with the brothers and everybody was in a warm and jovial spirit. The organist walked in and began giving the students the signal for the procession. They lined up, first by divisions and second by height.

"I now introduce to you the Douglass Class of 2004."

There was a deafening roar from the crowd and a standing ovation as two hundred proud African American students walked down the aisle. The graduation exercise included the Pledge of Allegiance, "Lift Every Voice and Sing" and an opening prayer. There were several songs, a welcoming address and a speech by the valedictorian and the salutatorian. After the special guest speaker, Mrs. Roberts came to the microphone and said, "And now the moment we have been waiting for. We now present the graduates. We ask that parents hold their applause until all graduates have received their diplomas."

The students giggled knowing that this request always went overlooked by the parents. The students expected that when they received their diplomas, their parents would take pictures and applaud for each of them. Every year it became a popularity contest of which graduate would receive the most applause; the winner would probably be the one who secured more than the four tickets allocated for each child. The Taylor family had 26 people present. Marlon had been used to waiting for his name to be called. He often wished his name was Marlon Allen or something starting with an A or a B so that his name could be called first. Oh well, he had waited four years, so 20 additional minutes wouldn't be catastrophic.

Finally, they concluded the S names and they move to the T's. Marlon was the first T to be called. There was a thunderous roar from the crowd. Four family members were down in front taking pictures. A gift-wrapped box was also given to him as he receives his diploma. Mrs. Sanders, one of the teachers, had to whisk Marlon down the stage because he was blocking traffic for the next graduate as he posed for more pictures. Marlon went back to his seat with a grin all over his face that said, I HAVE DONE IT! He was now a high school graduate. He had the diploma in his hands. He had a gift in his hand to remind him. He had 26 people in the audience who loved him He had a Lincoln stretch limousine waiting outside for him. He had the world at the tip of his fingers. He had his future in front of him. Marlon didn't remember what happened from that point on. He didn't know when the program ended.

He can't even remember when the graduates walked out. As they took their robes off, many of the students began to realize this might be the last time that they were going to see each other. Some were going to college, others to the military and some were going to look for employment. Marlon was so happy to have graduated from high school that neither he nor his family had thought about what he would do after graduation. He had plenty of time during the summer, he guessed, to figure that out. Many of the students said that they would stay in touch; maybe we'll get together for an annual picnic. Marlon ran out of the auditorium to spend the rest of the night with his family.

They had dinner reservations at one of the finest restaurants in town, and Marlon was going to enjoy riding in a limousine. This restaurant was primarily frequented by Whites and Blacks that were middle class, but tonight they were middle class and they had a reservation for twenty-six. Marlon couldn't remember a night as enjoyable as this. He enjoyed the ambience of the restaurant. He said, "This is the kind of life-style that I want for the rest of my life." Dinner concluded and the drive home was very festive. At 11:30 p.m. they arrived back at the Taylor house.

Everybody seemed pretty exhausted.

Mrs. Taylor walked into Marlon's room where he was lying on his back on the bed. She kissed him on the cheek and said, "I am very proud of you, my son." Marlon said, "Thank you, Mom. Thanks for being there all the times that I needed you."

When he woke up the following morning, he looked at his diploma and began wondering what he was going to do with the rest of his life. He asked himself, "What can I do with this diploma? Am I now an honorary citizen in the city? Will this diploma allow me to secure employment and take care of my family? Will this diploma get me a business?" He continued to look at the wall and wondered why today felt so different from yesterday. He wished that yesterday had never ended. He thought about all of his friends that entered high school with him as freshmen — some were dead, others were in jail, some were hanging out on corners selling drugs, others were working as stock clerks and a few were working at fast-food chains.

He wondered, "Will my future be any different from theirs?" They wanted him to drop out of school, but he always knew that he was going to finish. He and his mother exchanged promises that if he graduated, she would provide him with a special night that he would never forget. Now he doesn't want to forget it. He wants it to return, but it is no longer Sunday evening. It is now Monday morning. It is now Monday morning for an 18-year-old African American male with a high school diploma and nowhere to go.

There are thousands of Marlons around the country. There are thousand of African American males who are not incarcerated, who graduated from high school but have no future. For a myriad of reasons, college was not their first choice after graduation. For many, they needed to be convinced that there was an economic payoff to education. Many African American males have an attitude of, "Why don't I get this high school diploma and see what I can earn with it before I make an additional investment in college?" Many African American males know that a White boy with a high school diploma will earn more income than anyone else in America with a college degree. Most African American males are tired of a curriculum that is based on inaccurate information and irrelevant materials that are not applicable to their neighborhoods. Many are still wondering whether Columbus really did discover America. Did Abraham Lincoln really free the slaves? Regardless of whether it is true or not, what difference does it make if you live in the inner city of America?

For other African American males, they knew college was not financially feasible because their parents could not afford it and the government prefered paying for inmates rather than graduates. The joke on the streets was, commit a crime, go to jail, and while in jail, secure a college degree at the government's expense. A Black man has a much greater chance of getting an education in prison than from most American universities. Many African American males knew that their GPA and test scores were not high enough for acceptance.

Later in the week, Marlon began to write down the names of as many brothers that he could remember that entered with him four years ago as freshman, Next to the names of 75 brothers that graduated with him he wrote exactly what they were doing.

Of the seventy-five dropouts:

fifteen died,
fifteen were in prison,
fifteen were selling drugs,
fifteen were working in fast-food chains,
fifteen were underemployed: working sometimes, laid-off,
and in between jobs.

Of the seventy-five graduates:

twenty-five were in the military,
twenty-five went to college,
twenty-five are underemployed/unemployed/daydreaming.

Marlon giggled as he realized he was daydreaming.

What does White America want African American males to do after graduation? In Germany and Japan, there are excellent apprentice programs. Corporations sponsor these programs for the portion of their populations that will not attend college, because they are very important to their economics. The incentive to graduate from high school is economic stability for these Germans and Japanese. The American system seems to require a college degree. It is true that the American college system is considered the best in the world. This is borne out by the large numbers of immigrants that secure visas to complete their college studies in America. But for those who chose, for a multiplicity of reasons, not to attend college, 66 percent of the females and 74 percent of the males, being African American, what does White America want African Americans to do after high school graduation?

Does White America want African American males to go to a community college? If they attended or graduated from a community college, would they be gainfully employed upon securing their associate's degree? Is the objective to enroll in a community college and then go to a four-year school? Does America provide more financial aid for students after they secure their A.A. degree than after their high school diploma? Does America want African American male high school graduates to become legal entrepreneurs? Are there programs in

African American communities to identify capital and provide technical assistance for the development of business plans? Does the American public school system prepare African Americans to become entrepreneurs? Is the American public school curriculum designed for employees or for employers? Does White America need African Americans to apply at U.S. Steel, General Motors and Goodyear Rubber, etc.? Does White America want African American males to fly to Mexico and South Korea and other parts of the world where those plants now are and pay between 75 cents and $2.38 per hour? Does White America want African American males to work at fast-food chains, to clean hotels and other large corporate offices?

A friend of mine was telling me he had relocated from Los Angeles to Atlanta. His daughters were amazed and pleased to see large numbers of African Americans working in so many different occupations. What they were referring to was basic employment at restaurants, stores and hotels. Their experience in Los Angeles had been that Latino illegal aliens held most entry level positions and were paid below minimum wage. Does White America want African American male high school graduates to wash dishes, clean cars and pump gas? Those jobs have been replaced by microchips and robotic technology. Every time my car is washed at one of those automatic car washes, I still see Richard Pryor and seven other brothers who were working at the car wash. Each of those eight men was able to visit a young lady after work, take her out, and combining his meager wages with her salary, consider marriage and a family. When I go through the car wash now, I wonder, where those eight brothers are?

As much as I appreciate advances in technology, I'm still not convinced from an Africentric and humanitarian perspective that it is the most productive way to empower 250 million Americans. I am not convinced we have made progress if a factory which once employed a thousand people now, with robots and other computer operated machines, only employs 100 people. I am not convinced that America has produced economic options for the 900 "downsized" employees (Ujamaa vs. capitalism). I am very much aware that my value system is in conflict with theirs, because when they laid off 900 people, they were not concerned about what those people were going to do. Their only interest was the bottom line. If it meant reducing the labor force by means of automation or reducing the cost of e.g., labor by exporting jobs overseas, it was done.

If the value of humanity exceeds that of profit, then before we replace them with a robot, we need to provide options for the 900 laid-off employees. One of the contradictions with capitalism is that when 900 people are replaced with a robot, while costs have been reduced, robots don't buy products — people do. Who is going to buy their product? This forces American corporations to find new markets for their products.

Does White America want African Americans to stand on corners? There are laws now in some cities where if two or three people are gathered on a corner they are considered loiterers and are subject to fine or arrest. Does White America want African Americans to make babies and stay home with their children and receive welfare? Historically, welfare laws were designed to discourage males from staying at home. Does White America want African American males to join gangs, sell drugs and have access to guns to kill each other?

Marlon wants to know what does White America want him to do with the rest of his life. What is America going to do with African American males who have high school diplomas? Does America have a need for them? Does America have a need for African American males with college or graduate degrees?

I remember watching Minister Louis Farrakhan, on the Donahue show several years ago, and the issue came up about the 1.5 million African American males involved with the penal institution and the $18,000 to $38,000 that America spends annually, depending on the state, to incarcerate each of these brothers. This money comes primarily from middle-class taxpayers. Farrakhan looked out at the audience and said, "You know our track record. You know what Elijah Muhammad did with Malcolm. You know what we can do with these brothers. We can turn an addict into a minister, a criminal into a security officer in a housing development center. We can turn a brother that has never worked into a brother that will sell 1000 newspapers, 500 bean pies and 200 pounds of fish a week." He looked out to the audience and said, "White America, why don't you give them to us?"

You don't want them. You don't know what to do with them. You are spending billions of dollars to incarcerate them." And then he smiled at them and said, "And all we want is a couple of states." America doesn't mind sending African Americans to boot camp programs, but why won't America give these brothers to Minister Farrakhan and the Nation of Islam? If the objective is to balance the budget, wouldn't it be cheaper to give him Georgia or Alabama? What benefit does America gain in paying $18,000 to $38,000 per person for 1.5 million African Americans and the wasted productivity of the Marlon Taylor's, who are lying in bed or standing on corners wondering what to do with the rest of their lives?

Entropy and the Black Man's Predicament

There is a technological term, entropy, that relates to human behavior. Entropy is when a system, void of its essential maintenance resource e.g., energy, is deprived of the capacity to carry out its ascribed function. At this juncture the unit begins to disintegrate and ultimately dies. During this process, the disintegrating unit causes havoc as it becomes the hostile force, arbitrarily, capriciously and spontaneously bombarding other units, quite often causing damage and death to them before ultimately succumbing itself. When I first learned of this term and saw the parallel between what happens in technology and sociology, I began to see what happens in machines, where every machine part has a purpose, and if the part cannot achieve its purpose, then it will cause havoc for all other parts surrounding it. Unfortunately, it is the same thing with humans. Every human has a purpose, and if humans are unable to achieve their purpose, they too will cause havoc for all other people around them. The major purpose for men is to economically provide for and protect their family. If men are not allowed to provide for their family economically, they will begin to cause havoc for all other men around them while simultaneously causing damage to themselves. What does White America expect of the 75 members of Marlon's freshman class that did not graduate? What does White America expect them to do? What does White America expect Marlon to do if Marlon chooses not to go to college or the military since there are no internship and apprentice programs available? Can a man be a man in America without income? Can an unemployed man be a man in a patriarchal, capitalistic, materialistic economy? The major purpose for women is to give birth and nurture children. This remains viable and feasible for women.

The assumption that crime is based on need would imply that the poorest people in America should be more actively involved in crime. If that was the case, then Black women should be committing crime in greater numbers than anyone else. The reality is there are in excess of 1.5 million African American males that are in prison, while there are less than 70,000 African American women, or 10 percent of that total. The myth that crime is based on need could easily be dispelled with the reality that 80 percent of the crime in America is white collar crime—computer embezzlement and savings and loan scandals. A White male stockbroker embezzled $6 million and received a $5,500 fine. A Black male who was unemployed stole a TV set and received six years in jail. Crime is not based on need; crime is based on greed or power. African American men want the same power White men have. It is an unfortunate relationship in America that for every 1 percent increase in male unemployment there is a 4.3 percent increase in wife abuse. Why should these two factors, male unemployment and wife abuse, be correlated? The reverse is not true. Every one percent increase in female unemployment does not precipitate an increase in male abuse. It is obvious that the genders operate on two different value systems.

My wife and I were following the horror stories in Rwanda which the media did not want to place in a historical context. That's European imperialism. They divided the country into two warring factions before they physically left leaving hand-picked puppets in power who ensured the vitality of their oppressive value system.

My wife and I observed a commentator interviewing an African woman who had seven children. They had walked over 100 miles from Rwanda to the border of Zaire. In this very hilly terrain where very little grows, she was trying to stabilize her family for the evening and to get water. The commentator wanted to know why her husband and the father of the seven children was simply sitting next to the tree. My wife also wanted to know because you see the same behavior pattern among many African American men. She wanted to know what is it about manhood, specifically African manhood, that creates this tendency, whether in Rwanda or the United States. I asked a brother from Liberia, who I was doing some consulting work with, for his analysis. He said it's about pride. When African men have been able to provide for their families economically, and then they don't feel capable of doing that, it effects their psyche. For many of them it incapacitates them from doing whatever it takes to feed and clothe their children. In the United States you see the same pattern where both the man and the woman are working menial jobs. They are both subject to verbal abuse from White supervisors, but the woman remains there because she has mouths to feed at home. But many brothers get frustrated in that circumstance and walk away from their jobs. While I understand the issue of power and pride and ego, while I understand that in Los Angeles African Americans resent now being on the same totem pole as immigrants who just crossed the border and speak no English, while I understand that many of these businesses are taking advantage of the immigrants and paying them less than the minimum wage, I still believe that some income is better than no income. Legal work is better than illegal work. There is pride to be found in a good day's work. This may be the most pivotal issue men have to resolve.

In our crime watch group, we had a long discussion about that part of our race that is so frustrated about their economic options that they will either not work at all or choose illegal means to take care of themselves financially. Many older African American men don't understand the issues facing younger African American males. Many of these older men still remember the good old days when they arrived in the industrial belt in the 40s and 50s and jobs were plentiful. They remember when you could drop out of school at sixteen, or if you were like Marlon and graduated at eighteen, you could earn between $8 and $18 per hour. These men with very little education were able to provide a middle-class lifestyle for their families. When these men retired, their job and $18 per hour were not transferred to their sons. Corporations either closed the plant and opened one overseas, or hired part-time workers to avoid paying medical benefits. Unfortunately, the ideology and viewpoint of many older African American men does not reconcile itself to the present economy. Therefore, older population has a tremendous communication problem with younger African American males. I often remind these older brothers of stories where in Chicago e.g., there was a rumor that the Sheraton Hotel was looking to hire 5,000 people. The following morning 10,000 to 15,000 African Americans, mostly men, came looking for work in sub zero temperature. I don't know if those older brothers did that in the 1940s.

Within the context of the term, entropy, it has been said that your most productive economic years will be 20 years after your formal education. As Marlon lies in bed looking up at the ceiling wondering about his options, the theory says that his most productive, economic years will be between eighteen and thirty-eight. For his classmates who dropped out of school at sixteen, their most productive years will be between sixteen and thirty-six. When you look at African American males between the ages of 16 and 36, or between 18 and 38, unfortunately this is not the time when they are the most economically productive. This is the time, based on entropy, when they are most dangerous, not only to themselves (suicide), but to other people (homicide).

Many times principals give me the opportunity to speak just to their male students. It is a very humbling and tremendous experience to speak in front of 500 to 1,000 African American males between 14 and 19 years of age in high school. When I look at them, I see their potential, and I imagine what would happen if these 1,000 brothers could be converted to the liberation struggle and join organizations that give our community direction.

I look out at the audience and I see where these 16-year-old brothers will be 20 years from now. Statistics show that many will be dead via homicide, suicide or some type of accident. Others will be either using or dealing drugs. One-fourth will be in prison. Others will be marginally employed. I ask the Lord to allow them to see Him when they see me and allow me to give the best speech of my life.

My best experience was one where after I spoke the principal had organized 100 men that were going to break up into small groups with these boys to discuss my speech further over lunch. That gave the program more impact because there was immediate follow-up, but that's just one day. These boys need follow-up each and every day. I often dream that after I speak, I would have buses outside that would take thousands of African American males from this urban area to the country. In a safe environment, we would teach them Africentric manhood. They would return to the city at twenty-five years of age when they had mellowed out, when they were no longer dangerous, when they knew "whose" they were, "who" they were, who the enemy was and empowerment strategies.

The late author Amos Wilson in his book, *Black on Black Violence*, pointed out something that is very unfortunate in our community. Black men kill themselves with their futures ahead of them while White men do it when their futures are behind them. "One dies a blossoming in the Spring: the other after the first frost of Autumn. The Black man has packed all the guilt, failure, shame, fatalism, pain, hopelessness, and cynicism of a lifetime within a span of three decades. Somehow the cavalier optimism of youth and willful self-confidence of young manhood are dissipated at or before the point of actualization and assumptions of their powers to transform the world. Somehow Black youth and young adults are born into and come early to exist in a different ominous reality; one that was created for them; one under the control of others."[1]

That created "reality" negates, diminishes, and saps their will to live. It makes their lives pointless, an absurdity filled with bitter irony, happenstance and quicksand. Every effort at self-rescue seems to pull them more rapidly under, and every branch thrown to the sinking men breaks as they struggle to reach safe ground. The word *entropy*, remember, means that the nonfunctional, the useless part, will cause havoc not only for the parts around it but also for itself. That is why it becomes more and more difficult to distinguish Black homicide from Black suicide, which we will discuss in the following chapter in more detail.

Marlon is still waiting in his room trying to reconcile his Sunday night experience with his Monday morning reality. He has played the game the way the game was supposed to be played. He stayed in school for eight years of elementary school and four years of high school and he is now looking for the pot of gold at the end of the rainbow. Some African American males played the game an additional four years in college and are still waiting for the pot of gold at the end of the rainbow. Conformity is sold to White Americans. White Americans are convinced that if you follow the American rules, you can live the American dream. Unfortunately, nonconformity is now being sold to African Americans, specifically African American males. It used to be that youth believed that if you secured a good education and worked hard there would be an economic windfall at the end. Today our youth believe that nonconformity may be a more lucrative option. They have seen too many Marlons with high school diplomas hanging out on corners. They've seen too many brothers with college degrees who are still looking for employment. Many African Americans, especially African American males, now believe the better options are not in a better education and working hard but in a sports or rap contract, or a drug deal.

Ironically, the White version of Marlon across town also experienced graduation Sunday. Interestingly enough, both African American males and White American males will sell drugs. But the White Marlon's in this world will sell legal drugs. They will be from pharmaceutical companies; and he will be paid a base salary and commissions. I see these young men on airplanes frequently. These White males that did not finish college, and in some cases did not even start college, will make more than most African Americans with college degrees. Those White males who graduated from high school on Sunday night will now tell my mother and father what to do on Monday morning as they become vice-president of their daddy's firm.

It is obvious that African American males have the tenacity and an expertise in selling. Many of these drug dealers work ten, twelve, fourteen, twenty, twenty-four hours a day. They understand advertising, math and accounting. They will promote their product by giving it to you free to see if you like it.

They can convert kilos to grams to dollar bills without the use of a calculator. They are masters at the ability to collect outstanding debts. Any corporation could utilize those types of skills, if only these brothers had a legal product to sell. I commend Minister Farrahan, Father Michael Fleger and others who have given young brothers legal products to sell.

Do African American adults sell their future short when they say that they can't save the older youth, 14 to 19-year-olds, so they need to work on saving the children? I understand the statement. I am a strong advocate of correcting the problem before it develops and is exacerbated. I am an advocate of confronting the Fourth Grade Syndrome. I am a proponent of correcting the problem before the Fourth Grade Syndrome. I believe that the best time to intervene for African American males is fourth grade. It is more cost-effective at fourth grade than at 12th grade. But are we making that statement because it is the most feasible option or because we feel incapacitated and impotent as it relates to correcting the problem for our older youth? Are we making that statement because we have limited human and financial resources? Are we questioning God's ability to save these brothers between 14 and 19 years of age? Do we as adults feel so weak and helpless against the problems that are so acute and grave that we don't create the resources to save these brothers? If African American adults don't save these young men who will? If we save the youth between 9 and 13 years of age, what are we going to do with them when they become fourteen? Do we stay with this young group until they become adults? Do we take them to the countryside and bring them back to the city when they're thirty? Do we feel our resources are strong enough to work with youth between the ages of 9 and 13, or infancy to nine? Do we then release them to negative peer pressure, gangster rap, gang bangers, drug dealers and a hostile media? Do we think that what we do with these youth will undergird them against the upcoming onslaught of violence? Can African American adults sell the future to their children if they cannot save their youth between fourteen and twenty-one years of age?

W.E.B. Du Bois, in the early 1900s, stated that the major question of the 20th century was going to be the color question. Throughout that century he was correct. I believe it will continue into the twenty-first century, but I also believe that there is an additional question that may have an equal importance. And that is the question of economics; the major question of the twenty-first century will be the economic question. To be most succinct, the major question of the twenty-first century will be, How many people do you employ? The same question will be posed to the Black middle class and Du Bois's talented tenth. Maybe the reason why African American adults sell their future is because they don't employ their future.

The reason for the success of the Nation of Islam is that when they go into prisons they go in with more than ideas; they provide employment opportunities through basic goods and services. They sell suits, newspapers, bean pies, and security contracts. Amil Cabral taught that intellectuals discuss ideas, but the masses respond to basic goods and services. Are we as a race and a community going to succumb to entropy? Are we going to self-destruct? Does White America really believe that African American males that suffer entropy are simply going to stay silent in the ghetto and slowly die? These thoughts are addressed in Claude Brown's *Man Child in the Promised Land*, Richard Wright's *Native Son* and Nathan McCall's *Make Me Wanna Holler.*

This chapter has looked at Marlon's economic options with a diploma. The next chapter will describe the characteristics associated with manhood and the role of rites of passage programs in socializing our male youth.

Rites-Of-Passage comes from our rich African tradition.

$\mathscr{C}$HAPTER $\mathscr{N}$INE

Male Seasoning and Rites of Passage

Sekou Toure, president of Guinea, described a certain form of seasoning called the science of dehumanization. It is the process of indoctrinating you against yourself by denying internal development for external reward.[1] This chapter takes a look at men in general and African American men specifically whose poor communication skills, decline in academic interests and weak emotional development may be linked to the male seasoning process. First let us ask the question, What is a man? Goldberg, in his book *Hazards of Being Male*, writes that a man is

> an independent strong achiever who can be counted on to be always in control. His success in the working world is predicated on the repression of self and the display of controlled, deliberate, calculated, manipulative responsiveness. The man who "feels becomes inefficient because he gets emotionally involved and this inevitably slows him down and distracts him. His more dehumanized competition will then surely pass him by."[2]

The questions Michael Brown asks in *Image of a Man* provides a picture of manhood held by most African American male youth:

> How much pain or violence can you inflict on another person;
> How many girls can you impregnate and not get married;
> How much reefer you can smoke, pills you can drop, and wine you can drink;
> How many times you can go to jail and come out "un-rehabilitated",
> What kind of clothes you wear;
> How much money you have;
> What kind of car you drive.[3]

To the above, I will add the "classics." Men do not cry, ignore

125

symptoms of ill health, must bring home the bacon and do not display affection to anyone, especially their sons.

There has been much debate over the last decade concerning the significance of biological and sociological factors in male development. Genetically, males have X and Y chromosomes, while females have X chromosomes. Males have the hormone testosterone while the female hormone is estrogen.[4] The chemical makeup of the male body is 40 percent muscle, 15 percent fat; a woman's body is 23 percent muscle and 25 percent fat.[5] Some researchers use these differences to explain why men are more aggressive and excel in math and why women are more passive and excel in communication.

The debate becomes heated when other researchers point to society's role in encouraging aggression and math in boys, and passivity and communication in girls. The images of John Wayne and Rocky, along with the fact that men dominate the fields of math and science, provide role models which perpetuate the myth. Roger Brown, in his article "*Social Psychology*," paints the picture:

> In the United States a real boy climbs trees, disdains girls, dirties his knees, plays with soldiers, and takes blue for his favorite color. A real girl dresses dolls, jumps rope, plays hopscotch, and takes pink for her favorite color. When they go to school, real girls like English and music and "auditorium," real boys prefer manual training, gym and arithmetic. In college the boys smoke pipes, drink beer, and major in engineering or physics; the girls chew Juicy Fruit gum, drink cherry Cokes, and major in fine arts. The real boy matures into a man who plays poker, goes hunting, drinks brandy, and dies in the war; the real girl becomes a feminine woman who loves children, embroiders handkerchiefs, drinks weak tea, and "succumbs" to consumption.[6]

Experience has taught me that very little, if any, research is objective. The researcher brings to the subject his or her values and frames of reference. "His-story" is just that — someone's story about what happened. I originally sought to prove biologically why males are aggressive, which would explain why boys receive disproportionately harsh treatment in schools. I found literature documenting study after study to confirm biologically why males behave in a certain manner; I also found just as much literature either refuting the biological significance or raising strong doubts about the denial of sociological factors. It is my opinion that because the two factors, *nature* and *nurture*, cannot be separated for laboratory investigation, the debate is futile. I also feel that, while many researchers believe testosterone increases aggression in males (and I do not deny the possibility), honest researchers must admit that our sexist environment has clearly prescribed roles for men and women which perpetuate the gender stereotypes. I cannot state, then, that the reason boys, and specifically African Americans, perform at a lower level than their female counterparts is because they have testosterone, which produces aggression. I can say unequivocally that our society encourages males to release their aggression in contact sports such as football and boxing. Boys learn very early that disagreements can be settled with fists, while male-dominated governments clarify their disagreements with other nations by means of war.

This debate is similar to the left brain/right brain controversy, whereby the left hemisphere is very analytical and excels in math and science, while the right hemisphere is holistic and excels in communication, fine arts and sports.[7] In private academic circles, the notion exists that Europeans, and specifically men, are more left-brain oriented, and people of color, specifically women, are more right-brain oriented. The myth becomes a self-fulfilling prophecy if parents, teachers, counselors and the mass media provide the reinforcement. How can you separate biological theory from the social environment where it is manifested? The myths that African Americans are lazy, lack initiative, are super sexy, love to dance, sing and play basketball become self-fulfilling if role models and encouragement are not provided in other areas by parents, educators and community advocates.

Parents often perpetuate male seasoning by patterning their household to fit the sexist mold. Female parents, who are well aware of the lack of male support, can often be found rearing their male child with few household responsibilities required. Many boys continue to reach manhood with little skill and less interests in cooking and cleaning. Parents, educators and community advocates do little to reinforce the male child who has interests in the fine arts, religion and reading.

Some mothers demand less academic achievement, maturity and household chores from their sons than their daughters. Boys are also allowed later street hours, more sexual permissiveness and more athletic pursuits than their female counterparts. It is very difficult to be economically, emotionally, and domestically self-sufficient if academic mediocrity, nonattendance at spiritual activities, minimal intimate communication and exemption from household tasks are condoned.

The difference in child-rearing practices for sons and daughters has important implications for adult male-female relationships. Men may enter these relationships with fewer academic, economic, emotional and domestic skills. They may expect women to love them unconditionally and to be as loyal to them as their mothers are. Women who saw their mothers do everything without a man will be aggressive and more academically accomplished, as well as emotionally and domestically self-sufficient. A woman would like for her man to demonstrate these same qualities, but because of the way she has been raised, as opposed to the male track record, she often feels that it is in her best interest to keep a little money on the side, just in case.

It is hard to imagine the tremendous pressure on approximately 10 percent of the world's population (European men), who have the desire to rule the world. There are 6 billion people in the world, of whom 5.4 billion have color; only 600 million[8] (I am being generous with the U.N. estimates) lack color, or 10 percent. For the sake of simple math, I divided the 10 percent in half, although in actuality there are more European women than men. Perhaps we cannot imagine, having been oppressed for so long, the tremendous burden assumed in running the world. To be a "world runner" you must be macho, you must die with your boots on, you must never display emotion, never drop a tear. How can you run the world crying? On *Monday Night Football* the football superstar Emmitt Smith goes off the field with an injured knee, only to return later in the game to the announcer's cry, "Oh, what a man!"

The movie Making Love illustrates why the swelling number of homosexual men has reached an estimated 30 million in the United States. The two men in the movie shared their childhood experiences and their desire to be nurtured by a man, preferably their father. Unfortunately, men are not supposed to show affection and compassion to their sons, who need to be trained as future world runners. One man described his Little League baseball experience, in which his father worked with him all season on his hitting, and in the "big game," brought his friends to watch "his boy." The son did an excellent job at the plate, but late in the game dropped a flyball in right field. (The father forgot to teach him how to catch.) The father did not talk to him for a week and said he was too embarrassed to go to the office. Imagine the effect on the boy's psyche-irreparable damage, making him a prime candidate for homosexuality, as he still yearns for male companionship.

I also propose that this skeleton macho image of a man is a leading contributor to lesbianism. Can you imagine what happens to a little girl's psyche after being sexually abused by a sick man? Have we reached a point where men and women can no longer talk to each other with warmth and admiration? A recent article in a feminist magazine said that men listen less to women than each other, and women have a better chance for a conversation if they discuss what men initiate or if they talk to other women.

From both ends of the continuum, men seem to be blocked when they try to relate to each other. That is, they are not comfortable sharing their downsides, their failures, anxieties and disappointments. Perhaps they fear being seen as weak complaining losers or crybabies, a perception that threatens their masculine images. Nor do they seem to feel comfortable sharing their ecstasy or successes for fear of inciting competitive jealousies or appearing boastful. Consequently, verbal social interactions between men focus on neutral, largely impersonal subject matters such as automobiles, sports and politics.

Goldberg explains why being a male can be "hazardous to your health":

> When a man's self is hidden from everybody else. . .it
> seems also to become much hidden even from him-
> self and it permits disease and death to gnaw into his

substance without his clear knowledge. Autism, the severest form of childhood schizophrenia, runs three to four times as high for boys. In state and county mental hospital units for children, boys outnumber girls by approximately 150 percent. Under the age of fifteen, males are diagnosed as schizophrenics 42 percent more frequently than girls. Though there are approximately 105 male babies conceived for every 100 females, in the population at large there are today approximately 95 males for every 100 females. From birth on, the rate of attrition is significantly higher for the male. There are approximately 115 male fetal deaths for every 100 female fetal deaths. At nearly every age level, from birth to death, the male mortality rate is significantly higher. Specifically, from birth to age one the male death rate is 33 percent higher. From age fifteen through nineteen the male death rate is more than 150 percent higher. From age twenty to twenty-four, the male death rate is 200 percent higher and at almost all age levels after that, the male death rate is about 100 percent higher or twice as high as that of females. Today, the difference in life expectancy is four years and increasing (75 white men vs. 79 white women).[9]

European men need to recognize, for their own sakes, that running the world alone is not beneficial for their health, self-esteem or relationships with family and friends. It is unnatural for 20 percent of the population — actually, the 10 percent that are men — to want to control the world. African presidents do not want to control the world; they want to administer their countries. I believe this is correct, and justice will prevail. Unfortunately, Gil Scott-Heron, in his album Reflections, may be right when he says, "America was looking for a hero" and since John Wayne was no longer available, they settled for Ronald "Ray-gun."

It is equally unfortunate that African American men take their example of manhood from White men. Some African American men wish to dominate their women as Europeans dominate theirs, but because they do not hire and fire, and do not control the means of production, they become "aspiring chauvinists." Their dominance is expressed in the 82,000 rapes reported in the United States each year.

Again, African American men, like European men, are taught to be aggressive, to not cry, show little emotion and affection toward male children, ignore symptoms of ill health, and continue to bring home the bacon. African American men, though, have a difficult time bringing home the bacon, in contrast to their European counterparts. African American adult male unemployment hovers at 25 percent, and teenage unemployment is soaring to 75 percent, with a strong possibility that some will *never* work. Imagine what it is like in a male-controlled world to not be able to bring home the bacon. Is there any worse conspiracy than miseducation of African American boys so they will never compete in the economy? Liebow, in *Talley's Corner*, says:

> The way in which the man makes a living and the kind of living he makes have important consequences for how the man sees himself and is seen by others; and these, in turn, importantly shape his relationships with family members, lovers, friends and neighbors. Making a living takes on an overriding importance at marriage. Although he wants to get married, he hedges his commitment from the very beginning because he is afraid not of marriage itself, but of his own ability to carry out his responsibilities as a husband and father. His own father failed and had to "cut out" and the men he knows who have been or are married have also failed or are in the process of doing so. He has no evidence that he will not. The black menial worker remains a menial worker so that, after one, two or three years of marriage and many children, the man could not support his family from the very beginning and is even less able to support it as time goes on. The longer he works, the longer he is unable to live on what he makes. He has little vested interest in such a job and learns to treat it with the same contempt

held for it by the employer and society at large. From his point of view, the job is expendable; from the employer's point of view, he is. Sometimes he sits down and cries at the humiliation of it all. Sometimes he strikes out at her or the children with his fists, perhaps to lay hollow claim to being man of the house in the one way left open to him, or perhaps simply to inflict pain on this woman who bears witness to his failure as a husband and father and therefore as a man. Increasingly, he turns to the street corner where a shadow system of values constructed out of public fictions serves to accommodate just such men as he, permitting them to be men once again provided they do not look too closely at one another's credentials.[10]

The John Hopkins Research Center reported that for every one percent increase in unemployment, there is a 4.3 percent increase in mental patients, a 4.1 percent increase in suicide, a 5.7 percent increase in murders and a 4.0 percent increase in prisoners. The leading killers of African American men are heart disease, cancer, homicide, accidents and suicide.[11] African American boys outnumber African American girls 1.03 to 1.0 at birth, but upon reaching their eighteenth birthday, women outnumber the men 1.8 to 1.0. The life expectancy of African American men is 65, European men, 73, African American women, 75 and European women, 79.[12] These figures have much significance. African American men die before anybody else. (Legislation should be considered to excuse African American men from contributing to Social Security because they usually will not live to receive it!) European women live 12 years longer! African American women spend the last 10 years of their lives without their men, *if* their men are at home. The question of who will define manhood, seasoning, or rites of passage will be determined based on who spends the most time with our boys and who can attract and influence them most effectively.

Male seasoning thus becomes a dehumanization process of indoctrinating you against yourself; it is a conspiracy designed to make you a skeleton with no feelings and no compassion for your children, women or brothers. Psychologists have proven that expressing emotions can alleviate suicidal tendencies. Men returning home from work, or never going, sitting in rocking chairs with a beer all evening, never fully sharing with their spouse or children how they feel they're at risk of illness, depression and death. Men have become slaves to bringing home the bacon and letting mama bring home the emotion. It has often been said that being a man in America is very difficult, but I strongly advocate that we redefine manhood. Goldberg and Brown's description is not in our best interest. How can we build strong families and nations with a group of people who have not developed themselves internally? I believe manhood may be best expressed by telling your wife, "I appreciate you," by bringing your son to your chest, and by telling your brothers when you are hurting and need their help.

Let's review the messages that each group gives to our children:

Gangs, Dealers and the Media	**Parents, Teachers and Concerned Community Citizens**
2 to 8 hours spent together Increased involvement with age	7 to 34 minutes spent together
Active listening *to* each other	Aggressively talking *at* each other
Immediate gratification	Long-term gratification
Materialism, designer clothing, bright colors (large/flashy)	Internal, moral integrity and honesty
Money via drugs, sports, music, crime and the lottery	Money via a good education and hard work

    It should be obvious that we are not going to win against gangs, dealers and the media with fathers and mothers spending 7 and 34 minutes, respectively, and instructors spending 40 to 45 minutes disseminating irrelevant information to their youth. Many youth tell me that adults in the neighborhood don't even say hello. Many adults say they're afraid. Isn't it interesting that as our youth become older, they spend more time together, while their involvement with most adults declines.

    If you gave most adults an opportunity to make hundreds of thousands of dollars a day rather than giving years of service, many adults would probably choose the former. In *Motivating and Preparing Black Youth for Success*, I mentioned that for many of us life has been reduced to money. Our youth, via gangs, dealers and the media, have found five other ways to make money beside a good education and working hard. Our competition now has become drugs, sports, music, crime and the lottery. Needless to say, competing against these activities is difficult. However, we must make a good case for a good education and retirement security as opposed to the million-to-one odds of going to the NBA or the dangerous business of selling drugs. Ultimately, we must show youth that life is about more than making money. It's about finding something that you enjoy so much that you are willing to do it for free, but because you do it so well, you get paid for it. Adults must help young people identify and develop their talents and expose them to related careers. As a chess or basketball game, we need to design and carve out a strategy that will reclaim our youth.

    The media further complicates our efforts with its onslaught on our youth. Advertisers selling to youths is a major market, and youth often influence their parents' purchasing habits. The African American community is only 12 percent of the nation's population, but we consume 38 percent of the liquor and 39 percent of the cigarettes. Former U.S. Secretary of Health and Human Services Louis Sullivan, Rev. Calvin Butts, Father George Clements, Father Michael Pfleger and many others need to be commended for the strong stand they have taken in trying to reduce the consumption of nicotine, alcohol and hard drugs.

    Sullivan publicly reprimanded the tobacco industry for directly marketing cigarettes to Black males. Rev. Butts of

Abyssinia Church in New York along with the larger community, pressured billboard advertising companies to remove the billboards under threat of defacement. Father Clements, Father Pfleger, Dick Gregory and others organized themselves to make sure stores did not sell drug paraphernalia.

As an activity, I recommend that educators, concerned community citizens and parents cut out advertisements in magazines, cover up the company name and discuss with youths the messages that are really being advertised. Advertisements that appear to be selling liquor, cigarettes, and cosmetics are, in actuality, subliminally advertising a good time, sexual activity and materialism. The illusion is that smoking and drinking will improve your looks, provide a fancy car and make people of the opposite sex attracted to you.

Many of our youths' first encounters with smoking, drinking and sexual activity is during adolescence. A decision to start smoking at age 14 may very well lead to premature death at 34. A decision to become sexually active at age 14 produces a life long dependency on welfare. Some youths lack knowledge about their bodies, birth control and pregnancy. I have heard horror stories about youth who did not think that they could get pregnant during the first six months of sexual activity. Some youth who became pregnant thought that just as with other problems, time would remove it, and chose not to tell their parents. This miseducation will continue as long as the peer group spends more time with our children than we do. It really does take a whole village to raise a child.

There is also a need for adults to show African American adolescent males a way to resolve their problems through nonviolence. My staff at African American Images has designed a program called The Dr. King Nonviolence Laboratory. This project was established primarily for junior and senior high schools. The program teaches staff and/or students how to resolve conflict through nonviolence. Dr. King's theory does not need to be buried between 1929 and 1968. We need to show African American males how they can preserve their manhood without having to kill someone because their shoes were stepped on, they were brushed up against, their designer shoes or starter jackets were envied or they were just plain irritated.

135

The term "Black-on-Black crime" is often used by the media. We never hear the term "White-on-White crime." Any criminologist will tell you that crime usually takes place between people that are related, know each other or live nearby. Homicide is the leading killer of Black male adolescents; it is essential that we teach African American males how to resolve conflict through nonviolence means. In Chicago, there is a program in which 100 Black men volunteer on a regular basis to teach Black high school boys a strategy of nonviolence and conflict management.

An activity of our Dr. King laboratory includes role-playing. For example, two African American males brush up against one another and express themselves the way they normally would on the streets. Of course, we don't allow them to hit each other, but body language, hostility and all other expressions are released. We then bring them together as if it was the beginning of a boxing match. We have them look at each other, and in front of the group say that the reason why they hate their *brother* is that they hate *themselves*. We then expose them to Dr. King and his theories of nonviolence. If they must, groups can also consider allowing boys to resolve conflict through public competition: Indian wrestling, pushups or bench pressing.

Some Black boys think that talking back to their mothers, female teachers and the police is a form of manhood. We need programs and men that will teach Black boys the distinction between a battle and a war; it may be better to keep their mouths shut and lose the battle in order to be available for the war for the liberation of our people. The police often know how to bait Black boys into making a mistake. Too many African American males make a wisecrack or a wrong move and are shot by the police. Churches, schools and community groups need to establish a better relationship with the police so that we can reclaim our youth. Our males are being seized by the gangs, the dealers, the media, the police, and the penal institutions.

A professional organization called NOBLE (National Organization of Black Law Enforcement) attempts to organize African American superintendents, captains and other high-ranking officials around prevention rather than intervention. The relationship between the police department and the African American community will only deteriorate as more Black men are shot in the back. The relationship needs to be nurtured by an ongoing watchdog committee and NOBLE representatives. Efforts should be made, in spite of the affirmative action backlash, to increase the percentage of African American police officers to the percentage of African American people in the city. There are numerous cities where the African American population is 50 percent or more yet African American police officers constitute less than 20 percent of the staff and a smaller percentage of the officers. *This racial inequity* is further exacerbated in prisons across the state in rural areas miles from the African American community.

The Honorable Judge Eugene Pincham reported that 95 percent of the people who passed through his court did not possess a high school diploma, nor did they attend church while growing up. He and others have designed programs like Probate Challenge, which allows youth on probation to be given academic assistance, role models and cultural awareness. It provides a positive transition from probation to the real world. As 25 percent of our male population is involved with penal institutions and 47 percent of all inmates are African American, we need more programs like this. There is much that we can do for our boys. Many are angry.

For example, Darryl is 16 years of age; it's five o'clock in the afternoon; he's been outside on the streets since eleven o'clock that morning. There were a couple of times when he could have gotten high; he passed them up. There were opportunities to rob a store and steal a car. He robbed the store but chose not to steal the car. There was a chance to meet three females over someone's house when their parents were not home. He said he might check it out later that evening, and that he was going home to get something to eat.

He walked into the house and his mother (who was not home when he left at eleven o'clock) sort of looked at him and shook her head, while she continued to talk with her friend on the telephone. Darryl went into the kitchen, where there was nothing to eat. The mother then yelled, "Why did you come back in here anyway? Get your head out of that refrigerator. Sometimes I wish you were never born." Darryl stomped outside.

This is one example of the kind of male child on our streets, one who is angry, suffering from lack of nurturance and acceptance, and hungry for love. He gravitates toward his peers, gangs, young ladies that give him a two-minute thrill and drugs that may give him a short-term high.

There are also wayward boys in the White community. These boys don't always do their homework, don't always come home on time and are often involved with crime. In the typical White community, 16-year-old Joey has been acting up in the neighborhood, has thrown a couple of balls in neighbors' windows and has caused a minor disturbance in front of a dry cleaners and grocery store. One evening four or five White male adults, three of them business owners, and two concerned citizens decide to talk with Joey while he's idling away on the street. They tell him in no uncertain terms that they are not going to allow it. "We are going to give you a job at the dry cleaner's, and if you do well, we will find you another job at the plant or come up with some money to send you to college."

I call this the "safety net." When the home and school fails, children need a community safety net. In most communities, safety nets are spearheaded by the business sector. The business sector not only has the financial resources to respond but their commitment to its youth and desire to make sure their communities are safe for business growth and expansion is enormous. In the African American community, when the home and school break down, the lack of a safety net, whether by the church or the business sector, has increased the number of African American male youth that have become a threat to the people they encounter. I often tell people that while my father was my best role model, it was my track coach who created a safety net that prevented me from spending idle time on the streets.

We need businesses, churches, community organizations and concerned African American men to identify adolescent males and provide them with a safety net which includes direction, high expectations, employment opportunities and educational advancement. This may be one of the biggest weaknesses in our communities; our safety net is not strong due to the lack of business development and since these youth are not biologically ours but belong to the African village. It should be obvious that a single parent or, for that matter, parents, will not be as successful as a village in raising children.

The struggle has come down to adults against gangs for the minds of our children, and Rites of Passage organizations against gangs for the minds of our children. Jeff Fort, a major gang leader of the Chicago Blackstone Rangers, once told me, "We will always have the youth because we make them feel important." I'll never forget that. Fort is a gangbanger who understood psychology very well. One of the ways to attract people to an organization is to spend time with them and make them feel important. In that respect, the gangs do a very good job. It is now the responsibility of the adult community to also give our youth more of our time to make them feel important.

Fathers are not going to win the battle for our youth spending only seven minutes a day with their sons. Men are not going to capture the imagination of male youth when the Cub Scouts and Boy Scouts in many areas are now being administered by women. I don't believe that African American women want these positions, but they do want their sons in constructive activities. If men are not going to respond, then by default women will fill the void.

In Ray Raphael's book *The Men from the Boys*, he describes what it's like when urban male youth do not receive a clear definition of manhood:

> Traditional cultures throughout the world have often devised ways of dramatizing and ritualizing the passage into manhood and of transforming that passage into a community event. Through the use of structured initiation rites, these societies have been able to help and guide the youths through their period of developmental crisis. By formalizing the transition process, complex problems of identity formation are translated into concrete and straightforward tasks. Often, the trials a youth must endure are extreme:
>
> Throughout their journey, the elders belabored them with firebrands, sticks tipped with obsidian and nettles. They arrived covered with blood and were received by a pair of guardians. A period of seclusion followed, during which the boys had to undergo a series of trials. They were beaten, starved, deprived of sleep, partially suffocated, and almost roasted. Water was forbidden,

and if thirsty they had to chew sugar-cane. Only the coarsest foods were allowed, and even these were left raw. All the time the guardians gave them instructions about kinship, responsibilities, and duties to their seniors. At length, after some months, the priest summoned the supernatural monsters from the underground while the other men sounded the bull-roarers. The guardians now taught their charges how to incise the penis in order to eliminate the contamination resulting from association with the other sex. Subsequently, this operation had to be performed regularly. A series of great feasts then took place, and initiates emerged richly decorated.

This is how a Busama youth in the highlands of New Guinea proves his manhood. As odd as the rituals might sound to us, their impact is forceful and direct: If a youth can make it through this bizarre sequence of mutilation and deprivation, then certainly he can handle the everyday hardships he will confront throughout his adult life. Dramatically and emphatically, he has repudiated the vulnerability of boyhood while asserting the toughness and resilience required of in manhood. In his own eyes and in the eyes of society, he has shown himself to be worthy of adult respect.

Perhaps we have something to learn from this primitive Rites-of-Passage. The underlying structure of the ritual is enviable, even if the details might seem sordid. Listen, for example, to a typical reaction of a modern day man to the crude but gutsy Busama initiation rituals:

I wish I had it that easy. Run through the fire, step on the coals — then it's over and done with. You're a man, everyone knows you're man, and that's the end of it. For me it keeps on going on and on. The uncertainty of it — at any moment you can be out of the streets. It's all tied up with money. I've got to keep on fighting for money and respect. The fire never stops; I keep running through it every day.[13]

I have been actively involved over the years in assisting Rites-of-Passage organizations. We need them in every city, neighborhood, and every block. I discuss how to organize the adult male population, the need for study and bonding among this group, how to identify a facility, which recruitment strategies to use, the desired age range and the number of youth to be served.

The basic topics studied in most Rites-of-Passage programs include African and African American history, economics, politics, family responsibility, career development, spirituality, community involvement and organization, physical fitness and the Nguzo Saba value system, all taught from an Africentric perspective.

The objective is to have the youth master a predetermined criteria in these areas. Lesson plans are then designed to assist youth in this endeavor. The learning experience should be taught from a whole-brain approach rather than a left-brain approach. There is a strong tendency for African American men to do the same thing that teachers do in the classroom, which is to lecture the children or to pass out a ditto sheet. The use of right-brain activities, taking advantage of children's interest in music, fine arts, and the use of their hands, should be considered. I strongly suggest using our SETCLAE curriculum. The SETCLAE curriculum encompasses all of the above areas, so why reinvent the wheel? The following are sample topics and lesson plans:

African and African American History
- Develop a family tree.
- Design a time line from four million years B.C. through 2000 A.D.; indicate special events from the African American experience on the timeline.
- Read *Lessons From History: A Celebration in Blackness, The Autobiography of Malcolm X, Manchild in the Promised Land, Native Son, Kaffir Boy, Abdul and the Designer Tennis Shoes* and *Makes Me Wanna Holler.*
- Use raps, plays and debates, incorporating African and African American leaders into the material.

Economics
- Develop a family budget.
- Learn to read the stock pages.
- Create an example where a stock/mutual fund was purchased and monitor it over a period of time.
- Observe, analyze and write about the types of businesses and business activities in African American communities.

- Make a product or provide a service and sell it to the larger community, e.g., T-shirts, sweatshirts and memorabilia. Develop a business plan.

Politics
- Design a chart listing local representatives through the presidency with names and duties provided for each.
- Create a mock election, campaign speeches and debates.
- Arrange field trips to city, state, national and international offices, e.g., United Nations.
- Be involved in voter registration drives.

Family Responsibilities
- Require that parents design a list of chores and sign the sheet, confirming that the boy has completed these responsibilities.
- Provide classes in sex education; teach the difference between making a baby and taking care of a baby.
- Provide opportunities for boys to be involved in cooking, ironing, sewing and washing dishes. This can be done in an in-house session or at a camp site.
- Create an opportunity for boys to babysit infants and toddlers.
- Teach the boys carpentry and plumbing.

Career Development
- Have the youth provide five occupations for each letter of the alphabet.
- Invite guest speakers to talk about their careers.
- Provide tutorial services and awards ceremonies glorifying academic achievement.
- Review course schedules to ensure that career goals can be met.

Spirituality
- Teach the boys the three components of prayer:
    1. Thanksgiving
    2. Forgiveness of sin
    3. Request/Petitions
- Provide the opportunity for boys to pray.
- Review scriptures and have them memorized.

Community Involvement

- Have boys participate in community activities, cleanup drives, walk-a-thons, etc.
- Require a minimal number of hours to be volunteered in community organizations.
- Spend time with the homeless and in food distribution centers.

Physical Development

- Include the basic tenets of physical development, sit-ups, push-ups and running.
- Create sports contests and junior Olympics, martial arts training, drill performances (similar to the Nation of Islam and fraternities); teach health and nutrition.

Nguzo Saba

- UMOJA—unity: Teach the principle of operational unity. We may be discussing 10 items. We disagree on nine. In the spirit of operational unity we will work with the one area we agree on.
- KUJICHAGULIA—self-determination: Disallow the use of the word *can't*.
- UJIMA—collective work and responsibility: Prevent anyone from leaving any of the programs until all are finished with the activity.
- UJAMAA—cooperative economics: Pool all resources together in the purchasing of items.
- NIA—purpose: Assign every member of the Rites of Passage to declare a career goal and plan of action for achieving it.
- KUUMBA—creativity: Design T-shirts, jackets and caps in a very creative fashion.
- IMANI—faith: Teach and practice belief in God, prayer and scripture study.

In *The Orita for Black Youth*, by Frank Fair,[14] there are six basic requirements:

1. Understanding of the Black experience in America
2. Ability to manage the Family budget
3. Time volunteered with a community organization

4. Exploration of career and educational opportunities
5. Understanding the full responsibilities of citizenship
6. Study and application of biblical scriptures

In Nathan and Julia Hare's *"The Passage,"*[15] there are seven basic requirements:

1. Development of a log during the transition year
2. Awareness and understanding of self
3. Awareness and understanding of the immediate and extended family
4. Service to the neighborhood and community
5. Adoption of a senior citizen
6. Exploration of educational opportunities, including higher education
7. Development of discipline and responsibility

Both programs mandate that the youth be involved in the preparation of the ceremony. There is a great deal of similarity between the two programs, and while there are differences concerning economics, religion and elders, they do not preclude the Rites of Passage program from adapting those features they deem essential for manhood training. These models are just that, models, and are to be used to further inspire the cadres.

The word "Rites" is plural, meaning there are several stages of mastery. We advocate that the men design a structure which allows boys to matriculate through different stages, a process very similar to the Scouts, which had its origins in Africa.

In the African tradition, the Rites of Passage process starts with the naming ceremony and ends with a burial and becoming an ancestor. The general stages include the naming ceremony, the transition from boyhood to manhood, becoming an adult, and becoming an elder. All too often, mainstream programs serve children through the primary stages of development, only to drop them at the all important adolescent stage. By structuring the program to go from boyhood on up to elder status, 14-year-olds will be less likely to quit.

Because we are at work against the gangs for the minds of our youth, we must understand the significance of symbols. Our children value T-shirts, sweatshirts, jackets and caps. Rites of Passage organizations can provide these items with Africentric symbols to reinforce our culture and to create group solidarity.

There have been numerous success stories from Rites of Passage organizations nationwide. Some of the major pitfalls are men not remaining consistent in their interaction with the boys, parents who use the programs without giving support back to the organization and the fact that most Rites of Passage organizations are in the larger community while gangs are operating on every block. In the African community, all youth go through the same Rites of Passage. Consequently, all youth respect the process. In America, some youth have the fortunate opportunity to experience an Africentric Rites of Passage. However, when returning to their block, the boys may encounter gang members that do not acknowledge the experience, may resent it and may eventually retaliate against the youth. This does not negate the need for the Rites of Passage program; it simply reinforces the need for male consistency, parental involvement and more Rites of Passage programs to saturate the community.

To make sure you're on track, evaluate your Rites of Passage program with the following questions:

> Have our boys placed God first in their lives and allowed their decisions to be influenced by this relationship?
> How do our boys feel about their race?
> Do they have a tendency to hurt each other?
> How are our boys doing in reading and math achievement tests?
> Do our boys feel good about the school experience?
> How much time are our boys allowed to stay out?
> Who is the major influence on their decisions?
> Do our boys respect their parents, teachers and elders?
> Are our boys responsible for their allowance, their studies and their time?

The most frequent question that I receive from men is, How can they obtain more information about Rites of Passage? Many people want a manual or document that will show them how to develop Black boys into men.

In turn, I ask them four questions:

1. Have you read the Rites of Passage section in *Countering the Conspiracy to Destroy Black Boys* and *Coming of*

Age by Paul Hill?
2. Have you read respected Africentric authors who have written extensively about the Black male?
3. Have you changed your negative perceptions of Black men?
4. Have you worked out the program logistics, e.g., facility location, frequency of meetings and the target age of the group to be saved?

Black men tend to underestimate how difficult it is to organize a Rites of Passage program.

My experience has taught me that those programs organized prematurely around a manual, in contrast to those developing a cohesive cadre do not last long. There are Rites of Passage programs around the country operating with only one brother who is on the verge of burning out because he did not start methodically. Men must get to know one another and resolve ego and political issues before organizing the youth.

I am concerned that in our desire to save Black youth, we actually spend more time talking and reading *about* them, rather than in *directly working* with them. How many minutes do we actually spend working with youth rather than in study and discussion? It is not my desire to belittle theory, but theory without practice or an imbalance between the two is not productive.

The ultimate goal of Rites of Passage is to prepare the boys for manhood. Our boys do not know when they're men, and it is the responsibility of men to teach them. If men do not fulfill this responsibility, boys will continue to define it from a physical perspective, e.g., making a baby, fights and the consumption of drugs, alcohol, clothes and cars. Nathan and Julia Hare note,

> Boys reach physical puberty readily enough, but it is far more difficult, in an oppressive situation, to gain social puberty. We must recognize and actualize the difference between physical and social puberty in the Black boys' development, just as there is a difference between physical potency and social potency. Indeed, blocked from the avenues to social power and position, social potency, Black boys may too often feel impelled to overcompensate in the physical.[16]

The work becomes organizing a group of men who will study together, grow into a cohesive unit, identify a facility, determine the frequency of the meetings, identify and organize the target group of youth to be serviced, and consistently provide them with a program designed purposely to achieve these criteria. There are numerous reasons why some Rites of Passage programs have not been able to fulfill their goals. One of the reasons is adult inconsistency. One goal of Rites of Passage is to match youth with a role model. The smaller the ratio between youth and adult, the greater the process toward achieving the goal. When adults attend irregularly, it upsets continuity; and when they drop out completely, it puts a greater burden on the coordinator. Another factor is youth inconsistency. This results from age, parental involvement and other competitive alternatives. Nathan and Julia Hare proposed twelve as the target age.[17] Their argument is based on psychological and social principles, tradition and the reality that any age after this may be too late for intervention because of the peer group and a more physical approach to manhood. Many Rites of Passage programs service youth aged seven through nineteen. I don't disagree with the Hares' rationale, but I do understand the hesitancy some men have expressed: honoring a 12-year-old with the title of *man*.

Once again we return to the problem of decreasing involvement. Many parents let the upper-grade youth determine their participation. People complain that there's a shortage of youth programs, but I disagree. Parents are simply not insisting their boys' attendance. Rites of Passage and similar programs need the support of parents. Without parental support, children will be lured by the alternatives: sports, music, dating, peer groups and the mass media.

These inconsistencies, both adult and youth, provide less continuity and time on task to fulfill the rites of passage requirements. I would recommend that, besides addressing these issues, at least one man should be designated for each criteria. Often when the requirements are lumped together and no one is assigned a particular area, nothing is achieved. I propose that we draw from the high school graduation requirements model and designate that each youth satisfy each man's requirement in the particular area. This concrete approach will also lend stability because, while some adults and youth will be absent, the remaining people can continue fulfilling their objectives. This procedure encompasses the view that, while we would have liked to have carried a larger number of boys into manhood, we will concentrate on those in regular attendance.

Many Rites of Passage programs have learned from the scouts, gangs and fraternities, and have incorporated symbols, patches of achievement, T-shirts, sweaters, jackets and caps to heighten solidarity. While I have concerns about the overemphasis fraternities give to social activities and Greek culture, you have to be impressed with how the Omegas in particular, over a short period of time, can create a desire so strong that pledgers will be branded and swear to be a Q until the day they die.

I am reminded of the work of Marcus Garvey and Elijah Muhammad. These men turned "Reds" into "Malcolms" without governmental grants and doctorates in clinical psychology. They did it with hard work, a knowledge of their history and a belief in God. Nathan Hare shares that tradition:

I Am a Black Man

The evidence of anthropology now suggests that I, the Black man, am the original man, the first man to walk this vast imponderable earth. I, the Black man, am an African, the exotic single quintessence of a universal blackness. I have lost, by force, my land, my language, in essence, my life. I will seize it back so help me.

Toward that end, if necessary, I will crush the corners of the earth, and this world will surely tremble. Until I, the Black man, the first and original man can arm in arm with my woman, erect among the peoples of the universe a new society, humane to its cultural core, out of which at long last will emerge, as night moves into day, the first truly human being that the world has ever known.[18]

I believe a conspiracy has been designed to destroy Black boys. Black men must develop programs like Rites of Passage, which offers adult role models skill development, Black culture and a male socialization process that will lead into real manhood.

RITES OF PASSAGE PROGRAM

1. Organize a group of Black men willing to participate in the program.

2. Develop study sessions with this group discussing Black history and male development.

3. Identify a facility and decide the frequency and the length of the meetings with the young brothers. (Age is discretionary.)

4. The program should provide skill development, Black history, male socialization, recreation and "A Big Brother."

5. Recommended frequency of meetings is weekly, with one week allocated to a field trip, the study of Black history, the development of skills and rites of passage (male socialization).

6. Field trips should include prison, a drug abuse center, a teenage pregnancy center, a public hospital emergency room on Saturday evenings, a best high school honors class, the stock market, camping and computer oriented businesses.

7. The nine minimal national standards that all programs should include are spirituality, african history, economics, politics, career development, community involvement, physical development, family responsibility and values which could include the nguzo saba and maat.

The next chapter will explore the challenges African American men endure securing a college degree.

For the first time, we are facing a generation that will not surpass the educational attainment of the generation that spawned it.

*C*HAPTER *7*EN

African American Males on Campus

African Americans hold the unfortunate distinction of being the only group in America to have more males in prison than in college. There are approximately 1.5 million African American males in prison and over 609,000 African American males in college. Let me provide an overview of important statistics and trends interpreted from an Africentric perspective. Of the two million African American students in college, 1 percent, or 267,000, attend Black colleges. While Black colleges enroll only 16 percent of the total Black student body, they graduate over 30 percent. The overall retention rate for African American students is 43 percent, 41 percent for African American female college students, 53 percent for African American female college athletes. It is 33 percent for African American male students and 43 percent for African American male college athletes.

Listed below are the 50 colleges and universities that produced the largest number of African American graduates.

RANK	INSTITUTION	STATE	MEN	WOMEN	TOTAL	% Grad	% Ret
1	Howard University	DC	415	673	1088	78.6	46
2	Hampton University	VA	257	572	829	97.8	85
3	Southern Univ. - (Baton Rouge)	LA	280	445	725	92.5	25
4	N. Carolina Agricultural & Tech	NC	293	373	666	88.8	38
5	Grambling State University	LA	207	341	548	95.1	45
6	Jackson State University	MS	202	326	528	95.8	34
7	Wayne State University	MI	149	373	522	16.5	53
8	Univ. of the Dist. of Columbia	DC	225	272	497	87.8	34
9	FL Agric. & Mech. University	FL	146	317	463	79.0	33
10	North Carolina Central Univ.	NC	138	324	462	91.3	82
11	South Carolina State College	SC	179	280	459	92.2	52
12	Morgan State University	MD	158	299	457	92.0	16
13	Norfolk State University	VA	134	311	445	93.0	55
14	Chicago State University	IL	114	323	437	86.9	7
15	Univ. of Maryland College Park	MD	184	238	422	7.7	45
16	Prairie View A & M University	TX	190	231	421	79.7	25
17	Temple University	PA	113	274	387	11.1	24
18	Spelman College	GA	0	376	376	98.2	--
19	CUNY City College	NY	167	199	366	29.3	--
20	Rutgers Univ. New Brunswick	NJ	124	240	364	7.1	59
21	Tennessee State University	TN	132	227	359	69.6	39
22	Tuskegee University	AL	150	207	357	94.7	70
23	Southern IL Univ.-Carbondale	IL	203	142	345	7.5	5
24	Texas Southern University	TX	104	239	343	66.7	9
25	College of New Rochelle	NY	55	142	326	56.7	67
26	Virginia State University	VA	150	239	325	91.3	64
27	Morehouse College	GA	317	271	317	96.9	84
28	Univ. of S. Carolina at Columbia	SC	94	185	315	10.3	55
29	Bethune Cookman College	FL	87	0	306	93.9	34
30	CUNY Hunter College	NY	73	215	288	18.1	--
31	Memphis State University	TN	107	174	281	15.1	28
32	CUNY Bernard Baruch College	NY	98	180	278	16.1	--
33	Elizabeth City State University	NC	102	175	277	79.4	78
34	Winston-Salem State University	NC	89	188	277	83.7	68
35	Michigan State Univ.	MI	83	193	276	3.8	48
36	Alabama State Univ.	AL	93	182	275	79.9	N/A
37	N. Carolina St. Univ. at Raleigh	NC	115	160	275	8.1	40
38	Southern Univ. at New Orleans	LA	82	192	274	90.4	--
39	Univ. of California-Los Angeles	CA	100	173	273	5.2	54
40	Univ. of Arkansas-Pine Bluff	AR	90	176	266	85.3	--
41	Univ. of Maryland Univ. College	MD	105	161	266	15.4	--

RANK	INSTITUTION	STATE	MEN	WOMEN	TOTAL	% Grad	% Ret
42	University of Florida	F L	89	174	263	4.8	44
43	Xavier University	L A	70	192	262	84.2	--
44	Alcorn State University	MS	89	172	261	97.0	25
45	Univ. of California-Berkeley	C A	89	170	259	4.8	58
46	Univ. of N. Carolina at Chapel Hill	N C	87	165	252	7.1	59
47	Georgia State Univ.	GA	77	172	249	10.7	35
48	Alabama State Univ.	A L	77	169	246	97.6	16
49	Florida State Univ.	F L	84	160	244	5.0	39
50	Clark Atlanta Univ.	GA	70	172	242	98.4	80

With this quantitative data we can derive a qualitative and ethnographic analysis, with the emphasis and concentration being from the African American male perspective. I mentioned earlier that 26 percent of Black male high school graduates are attending college. In most large urban areas the dropout rate nears 50 percent. While I have seen figures saying that 80 percent of African American high school students graduate from high school, I don't trust school districts to follow the paper trail of students that have been expelled, pushed-out, transferred, etc. The first glaring problem I want to dissect is high school graduation rates. In a typically urban African American school, there are 200 entering freshmen. For purposes of simplicity 100 will be male and 100 will be female. To substantiate the 80 percent graduation rate, is to document that 80 males, and a total of 160 students, graduated from high school four to five years later. What makes it difficult for schools is that those 200 students that entered as freshmen might have graduated elsewhere. There is still some vagueness in terms of what the actual graduation rate is in large urban areas. The rates vary between 50 and 80 percent for African American males. For the sake of this analysis, with a thirty-point differential, it will be divided in half, and we will use the figure of 65 percent. It is at this point that we will become more personal and place an African American male in this scenario and walk him through the high school and college experience.

Our high school freshman is Jerome Brown. Jerome is attending an inner-city African American high school. There are 200 entering freshmen students; 100 male and 100 female. Four years later, the year of graduation, the class no longer has 200 students. With a 35 percent drop-out rate, or a 65 percent graduation rate, we lost 70 students, and there's a very good chance that we could have lost Jerome. Of the 70 students that we lost, using a ratio of two-thirds for the males and one-third for the females, we lost approximately 23 female students and 47 male students. So, instead of 100 males and 100 females, on graduation day we will have 53 males and 77 females. In simple math, there is a 50 percent chance that we will not see Jerome on graduation day from high school.

Because this chapter is looking at African American males in college, Jerome will represent one of the fortunate males that graduated from high school. Of the total population of 53 males, remember only 26 percent of that number will have the opportunity to attend college. Twenty-six percent of 53 equals a grand total of 14 male students of the 100 entering freshmen high school students that will be attending college. Remember, there are more African American males in prison than in college, and they are the only group that has more females attending than males. There will only be 14 males attending college, in comparison to 26 females, 33 percent of the 77 graduating. Of the 14 African American males that go to college, with a college graduation rate of 33 percent, approximately five of these students will graduate from college.

The odds are five percent that Jerome will enter high school as a freshman and become a college graduate. That is the grim probability facing African American males pursuing a college education. With those figures you begin to understand to some degree why African American males believe they have a better chance of selling drugs or securing a rap contract than they do of getting a college degree. In the following chapter economics and its impact on the African American male are discussed. I will assess Jerome's chances with a college degree of being gainfully employed and at what income level.

I thought it was very interesting that for both males and females, athletes had a higher graduation rate than regular students. For the female athlete, she had a 12 percent greater chance of graduating from college. The male had a 10 percent greater possibility. The image is that athletes cannot handle the rigors of college work. The reality is that they actually perform better. There are a myriad of factors intertwined in these statistics.

Contrary to popular belief, one of the major reasons why African American students don't graduate is not because of lack of academic preparation but the lack of financial resources. For some strange reason, many students that receive financial aid receive less with each passing year. The financial package is based on the premise that with each passing year of college the student will earn more income. I think the White establishment that designed this package were not aware that there are African American college graduates who are unemployed, so why should we assume that a college sophomore will earn more than a freshman and that a college junior will earn more than a sophomore and that a college senior will earn more than a college junior?

It is this faulty assumption that contributes to a low retention rate unless African American parents can help their children secure employment for internships where the salary is commensurate with their academic history. African Americans on athletic scholarships have a more secure financial base, which becomes one more reason why they graduate. In addition, there is a larger number of athletes on scholarships majoring in Physical Education. I am not belittling its academic rigor, but in my opinion, it is not as challenging as a degree in premed, accounting, chemistry or computer science.

Another reason for the low graduation rate among African American students is a feeling of loneliness and a lack of belonging on many campuses, especially White schools. College athletes benefit from having a coach, who is often African American even at a White school, who becomes a role model.

Another major reason for the low retention rate is the lack of discipline and time management. Many students who have additional responsibilities, e.g., athletics, employment and other extracurricular activities, ironically improve their GPA because they have less discretionary time available.

The issue of athletes at the collegiate level becomes more complex when you introduce Propositions 42, 48, 16 and 14. Each proposition demands a higher GPA and higher scores on the achievement tests. Many African American coaches feel it is unfair to have higher standards for athletes than for regular students. Secondly, the test has not been the best barometer of college success. The coaches are not compromising academics;

they want more weight placed on GPA rather than a biased test. African American coaches think athletic scholarships are an opportunity for African American males to attend college, an option which would otherwise be financially prohibitive. College scholarships should be denied to them by the NCAA before they have the opportunity to demonstrate their academic acumen.

On the other hand David Robinson, the late Arthur Ashe, and other athletes take the opposing view that it is not very demanding to earn a 2.0-2.2 GPA, a 16-18 on the ACT or 700-900 on the SAT. My major concern has been that the burden, as usual, is placed on the victim rather than on high school teachers, elementary school teachers and coaches. We expect the student athletes in the last two or three years of high school to eradicate ten years of miseducation. Those coaches that value academics and structure that into their program have been more effective. I don't think that it is an accident that schools like the University of North Carolina, Georgetown, Penn State, Duke, Providence College, LaSalle University, Boston College and Notre Dame graduate above 80 percent, and some in the high 90s. And there are other schools, such as University of Las Vegas, Texas at El Paso, Memphis State, the University of Louisville, Tennessee State, Texas Southern, Alabama State and Prairie View, that are 20 percent and below. It is obvious that some schools will admit you and other schools will help you graduate.

I admire and respect coach John Thompson formerly at Georgetown University. He thought that if Patrick Ewing in his four years at Georgetown could bring $12,000,000 to the university in terms of TV contracts, $11,940,000 was a pretty good return on the $60,000 investment on his four-year scholarship. John Thompson thought that the least that Georgetown could do was to provide a five-year scholarship, if necessary, tutorial service on the airplane and in the hotel and a counselor to monitor his progress. It did not surprise me to see Thompson following and giving advice to his star of 10 years during the NBA play-offs. Thompson remains his role model and as a result the bond remains. This is a major contribution to the higher graduation rate of the male athlete over the student that is not an athlete.

When I talk with students like Jerome and his girlfriend, Renee, on a typical college campus and I ask them the ratio between females and males on college campuses, they tell me it's 2 to 1. Many say it's 3 to 1, 4 to 1 or 5 to 1. When we actually look at the figures, we have 1.4 million African American females, which is 70 percent, and 609,000 African American males, which is 30 percent. This is slightly greater than a 2:1 ratio. The graduation rate is 41 percent for African American females and it's 25 percent for African American males; a 16-point differential. Yet when I ask people about the graduation figures, you get the impression that the figures multiply exponentially. Why is there a difference between perception and the statistical reality?

Many times sisters forget about the athletes when there are cultural activities. Unfortunately, many times athletes don't attend, either because of their schedule or lack of political consciousness. Maybe sisters and brothers forget about the male athletes when they tell me it's 3:1 female to male. When I speak on their campus, I may have 40 of the 70 sisters and only 10 of the 30 brothers, with 20 of the 30 being athletes. If brothers are involved with White women or women of other ethnic groups, oftentimes sisters will dismiss them from the population. Of course all of this is possible for females as well, but they're not as affected by athletics, political apathy, and interracial dating as African American males.

African American males who are studious, unfortunately can be accused of acting White, because they choose to be in the library instead of someone's dormitory room. They might also be eliminated from the ratio. If you refer to the table of the 50 colleges and universities that produced the most African American graduates, there is not one school that has more male graduates than female. This excludes, of course, Morehouse College, which does not admit females. This was the first year in which North Carolina A&T had a greater number of female graduates. But this year there were

157

373 African American female graduates to 293 African American males. A major reason why North Carolina A&T historically had a larger number of male graduates than female is that the emphasis was in engineering. African American males have fared better in engineering, as can be seen in the percentages of Tuskegee and Prairie View, which also concentrate in engineering.

My major desire in this chapter is to understand why Jerome and other African American males have a lower retention rate than their girlfriends. The retention rate is 41 percent for African American females and 33 percent for African American males. If it were not for a 10 percent higher retention rate for the African American male athlete and the disproportionate number of African American male students who receive athletic scholarships, the retention rate could be 20 percent.

Listed below are some questions to ponder regarding disparity.

- Do African American males experience greater institutional racism in college than African American females?

- Do they experience more racism at Black colleges?

- Do African American females possess greater discipline than African American males? If so, why?

- Do African American females manage their time better than African American males? If so, why?

- Do African American females have more African American role models on campus than African American males?

- Do African American females complete their assignments more often than African American males? If so, why?

- Are African American females more computer literate? If so, why?

- Do African American females utilize the concept of cooperative learning more effectively than African American males? If so, why?

- Are African American males more affected academically by their social life? If so, why?

- Are African American males affected more by their dating habits, which may involve more than one female at a time?

- Are African American females more focused, driven and goal-oriented? If so, why?

- Do African American males feel it is a more viable option to return home to their mothers than African American females? If so, why?

- Do African American women attend class more than African American males? If so, why?

- Do African American females study more than African American males? If so, why?

- Do African American males cram more than African American females? If so, why?

- Are African American males more affected by peer pressure? If so, why?

- Do African American males spend more time listening to music than African American females? If so, why?

- Are African American males more emotionally involved in pledging? If so, why?

- Are African American males more involved in the liberation struggle and Black Student Union than African American females? If so, why?

- Could the difference in retention be the result of a dynamic in which some mothers raise their daughters and love their sons?

- Do African American males spend more time getting high than African American females?

- Do African American males, excluding those on varsity teams, engage in more sports or get involved in more athletic activities than African American females?

- Are African American males more affected by car ownership than African American females?

- Do African American males spend more time visiting colleges than African American females?

- Are African American males more influenced by the option of earning money in illegal forms than African American women, e.g., selling drugs?

When you review these questions, which ones suggest external factors and which internal factors? Can racism be responsible for African American males not attending class? Or spending more time with their frat than with their books? Can the White man be responsible for a brother trying to figure out how he can date three sisters at the same time when he should be completing his ten-page paper in biology? How did the White man make African American men drink and snort more than African American women?

Please remember, I am the author of *Countering the Conspiracy to Destroy Black Boys*. I definitely know a conspiracy when I see one, and I am very much aware that it is not an accident that every president in this country has been a White male and that Black median income is only 61 percent of White median income. If you live in a world controlled by White men, then the greatest threat to Black men would come not from women but from other men. The best way to destroy the Black family is to destroy the Black man.

I definitely believe that there is something unfair and unjust and whatever word you want to use — conspiracy, happenstance, a strange occurrence — for the disproportionate number of African American males that are placed in special education, remedial reading and suspension. I am a strong believer in a conspiracy, but the reason why I wanted to write this chapter is because it is not the only factor affecting African American males' lower retention rate. Jacqueline Fleming, in her book *Blacks in College* points out that African American males do far better at Black colleges than they do at White Colleges. She too had a very difficult time trying to explain what the differences are, because both Black males and females suffer being in hostile environments, but it seems to affect the male more. Studies also point out that African American females at White schools or Black schools suffer at the White school because of the hostility, overt and institutional forms of racism. But at Black colleges, African American males seem to do far better, because they feel more confident about being able to secure leadership positions, Fleming points out:

> Since black, as well as white, males are similarly deprived, they are predisposed to interact competitively. The racial difference serves to intensify the basically hostile nature of male-male interactions. Black males have been excluded from participation in a wide range of activities and restricted to small groups of all black social and political organizations. Apparently, the restricted role that black males play, both within the classroom and without, acts to constrict intellectual gains that issue from being an actor in campus events. Upon entering what is in some sense alien territory, black males fall into the category of sub-dominant males by virtue of their visibility and small numbers. Interestingly, observers of primate animal hierarchies find that sub-dominate males lapse into a non-confrontational, lethargic state of behavior that can only be described as depression. In many ways the developmental profiles of black males in white colleges can also be described as depressed. They become unhappy with college life, they feel that they have been treated unfairly, they display academic de-motivation and think less of their abilities. They profess losses of energy and cease to be able to enjoy competitive activities. To be sure, there are ways in which these males do act depressed in as much as they become assertive and they participate energetically in certain campus activities. Nonetheless, these developments are defensive and do little to remedy their plight. Black men often try to work the problem out through their interpersonal lives. They may try to attach dominance over women or live through children. In black colleges, which offer so many opportunities for social ascendants, these interpersonal strains can be ignored.

If Black women suppress their assertive selves to please men, then we can understand why it is easier for them to develop their assertive abilities on white campuses. The data indicates that most predominately white college campuses there are few black men, especially among seniors. Furthermore, we know that on predominately white campuses black males are often undergoing depressive reactions that cause them to withdraw academically and psychologically. In other words, they are not men enjoying dominance, social ascendence or their own assertive abilities. In this context black women may very well be able to develop their assertive capabilities that help them hold their own intellectually.[1]

I remember when I was in college, and there were 1,000 African American students that were freshmen, and four years later, only 254 of us graduated. I knew that we did not graduate because we were smarter; it was a result of discipline, time management, study time, attending class, avoiding cramming, studying together, and utilizing tutors. If you look at the 609,000 African American males in college and the retention rate of 25 percent, that means there are 457,000 African American males that are not going to graduate. I wonder, will they ever go back to college? Will they ever achieve their goal? What is the state of their psyche? At what level is their self-esteem?

It was difficult getting Jerome from high school into college. I worry whether Jerome will be in the category of the 457,000 that did not graduate or the 152,000 that did. I don't like what I see when I witness Black male failure. I have spoken in cities where the coordinator points out to me, as we drive by, African American males standing on the corners, who were star athletes. These athletes knew they were going pro and receiving million dollar contracts, but unfortunately did not make it and are now busboys in restaurants and still talking trash on the corner about how they were one step away from becoming a multimillionaire. I am concerned about African American males that drop out of college for financial reasons and end up working at menial jobs.

My parents both worked for the post office and they observed numerous college students working there. Because the money was good, some left college voluntarily or because they were forced to, and they continued working at the post office. For that reason, my parents did not allow me to work there. Langston Hughes raises the question in his poem, "What happens to a dream deferred?" I often ask African American students what their majors are. Invariably the five most popular majors are business, computer science, communications, criminal justice and accounting. The African American community has so many problems that all majors are welcome and necessary. Unfortunately, there are very few African Americans, specifically males, majoring in education. African American children are 17 percent of the children in public schools nationwide, but only 1.2 percent are African American males. There are several states and over 20 colleges that have special scholarships for African American males who will agree to teach for several years.

The next chapter will try to explain why Marlon and Jerome's friends are killing each other.

Why do Black Men Kill Black Men?

CHAPTER ELEVEN

Why Do Black Men Kill Black Men?

"The Lord will let the people be governed by immature boys. Everyone will take advantage of everyone else. Young people will not respect their elders. And worthless people will not respect their superiors." Isaiah 3: 4-5   Good News Edition.

When you read that Scripture you wonder if you are reading today's newspaper rather than something written two thousand years ago. Communities are now controlled by boys, and young people do not respect their elders. This is the first generation of African Americans that does not respect their elders. It is the first generation of elders who are afraid of their children. There are parents who are afraid of their children. Parents say they do not know what to do with them. There are housing developments where there are few, if any, men. There used to be parks where if boys got into an argument and a fight ensued, there were men in the park who would break it up. Today there are parks where there are 300 children and there may not be one male present. Immature boys now distribute justice and determine right from wrong and decide who may have to pay with their lives. In Baltimore, like so many cities where we have ethnic enclaves, there is a neighborhood called Little Italy. On the other side of the street is the African American community, sometimes called a ghetto. Little Italy is a working-class neighborhood, with manicured lawns, populated by Italians. There is very little crime in Little Italy. If there is an act of violence in Little Italy, it becomes a newsworthy event. The media often find out about crime in Little Italy after the men of Little Italy have already resolved it. Please note, I said the men of Little Italy, not the police of Baltimore. Little Italy has very little crime, not because of extra police that walk the streets, not because they have an incestuous relationship with City Hall, but because Italian men have taught Italian boys the importance of the community and of what is allowed and not allowed to take place there. In Little Italy it is not surprising to see women by themselves, including elderly women, walking the streets late at night and not being bothered; in fact they might be asked if they want an escort home. Across the street in the African American neighborhood, anything and everything is allowed to take place and only the bizarre is reported by the media.

Consequently, if someone is shot in the Black community across from Little Italy, that might not be newsworthy because it happens daily. Maybe if three to five people are shot, or maybe if a White person was violated in the Black community the media will cover the story. But as long as it's the indigenous residents, then it may not be reported.

If a Black woman was walking down the street alone late at night and someone was walking toward her, she would probably prefer that the person walking toward her be a Black woman first, a White woman second, a White male third. If it's late at night in this neighborhood, she would prefer the Black male last. If you asked an Italian woman in Little Italy, if she was walking down the street late at night and someone was walking toward her, her first choice would be the Italian man, then the Italian woman, the Black woman third, and the Black male last. In the Italian community, her man was desired first, while in the Black community he was sought last. I could write a book dissecting the differences between Little Italy and the Black community because those differences illuminate problems, causes and solutions.

Why do you think Little Italy is different from the Black community? Little Italy could also be Little Chinatown, Little Korea or Little Arabia. It is unfair to compare a community of immigrants who voluntarily came to America with their culture intact with a group of people that were forced to come here and had their culture stolen. Culture is very important; it is your racial DNA. It gives you a sense of history, a blueprint for living and direction for the future. Culture is far more than food, dress and music. Culture is synonymous with lifestyle, values, history, purpose and direction. A people without their culture are a people without a past, present and future. A people without their culture do not know how to live. A people without their culture are no longer a people and they will act like animals. A people without their culture will be afraid of each other and won't trust each other. They will not pool their resources to start their own businesses or to support those that exist. A people without their culture will be afraid to walk down the street at three o'clock in the morning and meet someone that looks like them because the person that looks like them may not share their value system—their culture. People without a culture, people without values, are dangerous.

Little Italy, Little Chinatown, Little Korea and Little Arabia are different, not because they receive additional police support but because they have an intact culture. Their culture drives them to become economically self-sufficient and gives their boys and girls rites of passage.

Two excellent books that describe life in African American communities, where culture is often nonexistent, are *Do or Die*, by Leon Bing, and *Monster: The Autobiography of a L.A. Gang Member*, by "Monster" Cody Scott, whose African name is now Sanyika Shakur. He says in the book, "If I had been born in '53 instead of '63, I would have been a Black Panther. If I had been born in Germany in the early '30s, I would have probably joined the Nationalist Socialist Party. If I had been born Jewish, I would have joined the Jewish Defense League because I have the energy, the vitality to be part of something with power, either constructive or destructive. And because there was a destructive element around me when I was growing up, I went into the Crypts."[1]

Cody Scott described how important it was being in a gang. He compared shooting someone with an orgasm; it gave a sense of power. My gun became the great equalizer.[2]

I have noticed in my travels around the world, whether I am in New York, Chicago, Los Angeles, Toronto, Haiti, Jamaica, London, Botswana, Egypt or Ghana, African men love standing on corners. I have often wondered why brothers love hanging out on corners. Are they waiting for their picture to be taken? Do they want people to see them? What is it they want people to see? Are they afraid that they are going to miss something if they are inside and not on the corner? What do they expect to see? Who drives by those corners? And as Monster

Cody says in his book, it's something about the nighttime that makes corners more exciting; and we control the night.

In my research, I have found that 95 percent of the boys in jail were on the corners between 10 p.m. and 3 a.m. That is why I encourage parents, if you can't control any other time, to control this time span. I was taught that once you know the time and the place you have increased your chances of victory. We know the place is the corner and we know the time is between 10 p.m. and 3 a.m. We need to also understand the root reason why African American men hang out on the corner. Why is it that you see more African American men on corners than African American women? Why do corners provide a greater excitement, intrigue, and mystique for men than women? Monsters' favorite phrase was "putting work in for the gang." His choice of words was very similar to that of my father, who said he was putting in work at the post office. I knew that meant eight-ten hours per day, and Cody meant the same thing with the Crypts. Gangbanging became a full-time job, and his shift started at 8 p.m., and ended at 4 a.m.

The corner becomes more important if it becomes an issue of turf. If we have two rival forces, then, just like countries that are involved in military combat, each group has to protect their turf. If we add drugs to the equation, we have to protect turf because it's a distribution center. This strategy is similar for Coca Cola or Pepsi or any other corporation protecting their distribution system. In past generations, young males grew up, left the gang, and secured a job. Brothers are hanging out on corners longer because the jobs are unavailable. While mothers would prefer their sons to play outside, for many African American males life has to be lived inside. When life has to be lived in seclusion, if they can't walk down the street as they do in Little Italy, then many men feel they have already died.

I am also grappling with the question, why do Black men kill Black men? Why don't they kill White men? Why do Black men kill Black men more than Black women? Why don't Black men protect Black women? Why don't they protect Black children? Why don't they protect Black elders? Why don't Black males protect their turf from foreign businesses? Could the reason that African American men don't protect Black women be because no one taught them to do that? Could the reason that Black men don't protect their elders be because no one taught them to do that? Could the reason that Black men don't protect Black children be because they have not been taught to do that? Could the reason why Black men don't keep foreign businesses out of their neighborhood be because they have not been taught to do that? Could the reason that Black men do not kill White people be because they have not been taught to do that? Could the reason why Black men kill Black men be because that is what they have been taught to do? Nathan McCall writes in *Makes Me Wanna Holler* that he received 30 days in jail for almost killing a Black man and received 12 years in jail for robbing a White store with no injuries. Was he taught something? Had he been taught to devalue Black male life that day? There is a powerful scene in the movie *Juice* between Tupac and his adversary at their locker. Tupac is on the run and tells his adversary that he isn't — and that if he isn't — then you ain't —. And if I hate myself, you know what I think of you.

Amos Wilson describes this in *Understanding Black Adolescent Male Violence*:

> A sense of powerlessness and inter-personal violence are inextricably intertwined. Absolute powerlessness as well as absolute power corrupts. For violence has its breeding ground in impotence and apathy. True, aggression has been so often and so regularly escalated into violence. What is not seen is that the state of powerlessness which leads to apathy which can be produced by the above plans or the uprooting of aggression, is the source of violence. As we make people powerless, we promote their violence rather than its control. Deeds of violence in our society are performed largely by those trying to establish their self-esteem, to defend their self-image and to demonstrate that they too are significant. Regardless of how derailed or wrongly used these motivations

express it, they are still the manifestation of positive interpersonal needs. We cannot ignore the fact that no matter how difficult their redirection might be, these needs, themselves, are potentially constructive. Violence arises not out of superfluity of power, but out of powerlessness. Violence is the expression of impotence. Having accepted the notion promulgated by his white oppressors—that he will never measure up to their "projected as universal" standards, never be "as good" as they—he vindictively asserts that they will never be as "bad" as he. Thus, he finds near erotic delight in demonstrating himself as the "baddest" whoever. In this game he has a better than sporting chance to win; in this game he makes the rules. The essence of the black on black criminal is self-hatred or self-alienation. These can only be learned. Self-hatred can only occur as a result of the self having been made to appear to be hateful, ugly, degrading, rejected, associated with pain, non-existent or devoid of meaning, and adherently inferior. Such appearances and associations are the fruits of white American narcissistic racist projection against the African American community.[3]

Why do Black men kill Black men? Because their anger and frustration is displaced.

Again Wilson provides the clue:

Frustration can and does produce a number of consequences of which hostile aggression is only one. Generally, the hostile aggressive reactions to frustrations may be of two types—direct and displaced. Direct hostile aggression refers to the situation wherein reactionary aggression is focused directly against the perceived cause and source of frustration. Should the cause or source remain hidden, ambiguous, intangible, or more commonly, so powerful that a hostile, aggressive attack against it would expose the attacker to severely painful retaliatory injuries, deprivation, injurious loss of the various types and possible annihilation, that attack may be redirected towards some object, person, or group other than the original cause or source of frustration. This type of redirected hostile aggression is referred to as displaced hostile aggression. In this instance, the aggressive individual or party, pressed by anger and compelling need to express that anger yet constrained from expressing it directly finds partial release by attacking a less dangerous target.

Why do Black men kill Black men? Because they are afraid and are not allowed to kill White people. Why do Black men kill Black men? Because that's what they are allowed to do. That's what they are taught to do and there are few consequences. They are encouraged and given more guns and lighter sentences.

Why don't Black men protect Black women, elders, and children? Because they have not been taught to do that. They have been taught to hate themselves. Their anger cannot be converted to love unless they are taught their culture. It is very difficult, if not impossible, to love and protect someone until you first love yourself.

Earlier in the chapter in reference to "Monster," we said that a male living in a particular neighborhood could become either a Black Panther, a Nazi, a member of the JDL (Jewish Defense League), or Crypt—that he was a chameleon who could become whatever the community wanted him to become. That reminds me of when King marched on Washington in 1963 and there was a reduction of crime that day. It reminds me of Huey Newton and the Black Panther party in Oakland, and in that neighborhood where the Panthers were stronger, there also was a reduction in crime. When Nelson Mandela first visited New York there was also a reduction of crime in Brooklyn and Harlem.

It inspires me and lets me know that there is hope for saving our youth. Our youth are chameleons and they will be whatever we want them to be. Cody Scott, who was once known as "Monster," has now become Sanyika Shakur, and the only variable that changed was culture; rather than being a Crypt with displaced aggression, he is now a member of the Republic of

Africa and now understands the enemy. The White establishment is cognizant of his consciousness and they have placed him in solitary confinement. As long as he was "Monster," there was complete access to all inmates, so that he could teach them killing techniques.

In my earlier book, *Hip-Hop versus Maat*, I mention the killing exercise where we asked boys in South Central why they would kill someone. People that are sane agree on those items they would kill and die for. People who are insane have far more reasons why they would kill someone than die for them. We mentioned that they gave us thirty-seven reasons why they would kill somebody. Things as insignificant as—because he looked at me, he stepped on my shoe, ate one of my french fries, said hello to my lady, I just didn't like him—and they went on and on. Then we asked which ones would you die for, and they wanted to retract them, but we said, No. "What you would kill for is what you would die for."

We have said that African American men kill themselves with their futures ahead of them, while White men kill themselves with their futures behind them. Many times the police assume that any brothers that are together must be a gang, any act of violence has to be gang violence, any crime has to be drug related and their next incorrect assumption is that any death has to be homicide. For many African American males, you can't tell the difference between homicide and suicide. Amos Wilson provides the analysis:

> Through committing homicide, the black on black criminal steeped in his existential, internalized white supremacist instigated guilt, often seeks his own death; he desperately searches for his execution. He provokes others to do what he, himself, did not do that to kill him as a way to kill himself as a way of committing suicide. He is determined that his subliminal guilt must not go unpunished. So he placed himself in harm's way. He compels himself to live dangerously. He falls for the ultimate sting. Carrying another man's guilt, he pretends to live without it. He thinks of himself as a black pantherized predator, when in reality he has been chumped into playing the part of the sacrificial lamb.[5]

"When African American males drive away from the police in a hundred mile per hour chase and end up driving into a pole, was than an automobile accident or was that suicide?" When you have three or four macho brothers who think that they are going to be able to defeat forty gang members in shoot-out, should the police record that as a homicide or a suicide? When an opposing gang member walks in rival gang turf, knowing that there is a war going on, should that be recorded as a homicide or a suicide? When African American males are racing each other down congested expressways at one hundred miles per hour and there is a car crash, should that be recorded as an accident or suicide? Of all the African American males who O.D. on heroin and cocaine, should all those be registered as drug-related deaths or do you think that some of those could have been suicide?

One of the most challenging questions I have had to answer was, How do you convince a young person to value long-term gratification when he believes in short-term gratification, when he is aware that the life expectancy of a gang member or drug dealer is 19 years? One of the reasons why many middle-class adults have failed in counseling our youth is that they are using long-term gratification as an incentive. If you're not confident of living past retirement, you may not want to stay in school learning about Columbus, Lincoln and Washington. If your life expectancy is only nineteen years, you may not want to work at McDonald's for $4.35 per hour until you die. If your life expectancy is nineteen years, you may not want to save your money and buy a Toyota, Chevrolet, Ford or Honda when you can steal a Lexus and drive it this weekend.

What do you say to a Monster who is already eighteen and has one more year to live? What do you say to someone who has already tested positive for HIV? I observed an entire class that was tested for HIV and almost one-third of the class tested positive. People who hate themselves don't have much compassion for people with whom they are sexually involved. I have heard angry White male homosexuals who were angry at the realization that they were going to die and wanted to take as many people as possible to hell with them. The last chapter will provide solutions to counter this conspiracy against our males.

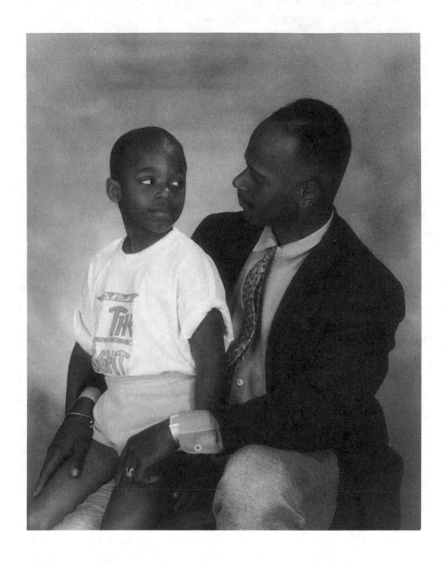

We can save African American boys with conscious, consistent, African American men.

$\mathcal{C}$HAPTER $\mathcal{T}$WELVE

Counter Conspiracy Solutions

Here are some case studies that have been based on actual experiences.

Case Study I

Ron Gilliam is entering his fourth year of college and has hopes of being drafted as a running back by the pros. Ron has won numerous awards as an athlete, dating back to his middle school playing days. I asked Ron how he was able to stay in school when so many of his friends had either dropped out or were pushed out. "I liked playing ball, and there was more competition playing school ball than sandlot and park district. I didn't like school very much, but looked forward to 3:15 p.m. when practice started," said Ron. "They held me back a year in elementary school, but I knew they couldn't hold me back a second year because I would be 15-years-old. Some of my friends said I was a better ballplayer than anybody else in middle school because I was older and bigger. I was determined to show them in high school, where the upperclassmen were larger and older, that I was good."

Ron was happy to know some high school coaches occasionally watched his team play. "Sometimes the high school coach would watch the middle school team play. I heard he asked about me and when they expected me to graduate. I knew then I was going to graduate, but maybe not on time," he said. "A lot of my friends played ball after school, but it was in the park or around the house. For some reason sports didn't have the same effect on them. Most of them dropped out around their sophomore year because they didn't like the teacher or vice versa." Ron continued. "I knew how they felt because they were in remedial classes with the dumb people, and it was embarrassing. I knew I wasn't bright, but I persevered for practice, and then I became a star. I knew if I could endure 9 a.m. to 3 p.m., I could go to the pros. Playing ball was always easier than diagramming sentences."

He added, "My high school coach only had to talk twice to my teacher about changing my grades. He always felt the best way was to develop my schedule, giving me a light, easy load and going to summer school each year. My college coach used the same procedure. I don't know what I'll do if I don't get drafted. I don't have enough hours to graduate, and hadn't thought about any other career except running back. I feel pretty good. I didn't drop out, I graduated from elementary school and high school. I'm in college, and one telephone call away from the NFL, concluded Ron."

Case Study II

Lawrence Drew has just graduated from elementary school as the top student in the class. He has big plans for repeating this feat in high school, earning a college scholarship, and becoming a doctor. Lawrence has a strong mother, Cynthia, who runs a tight ship. She is a single parent; she was divorced when he was five years old. Lawrence may see his father once a year. The mother is an accountant, and has been taking courses over the past three years in hopes of becoming a Certified Public Accountant. I had the opportunity to visit them one evening, and asked about Lawrence's success. Cynthia responded, "Nothing but the Lord. I pray constantly, because the streets are so dangerous. Lawrence calls me at work when he gets home from school. He knows to do his homework first; if he does not have any, or not enough for an hour, I bought him workbooks to supplement it. He can watch television, but for only two hours each day. We also have one hour for reading a library book of his choice. He writes a paper about the book that is due before he goes rollerskating on Saturday. We read the Bible daily, and attend church regularly."

I asked Lawrence, who is very quiet, if he could explain his success. Lawrence added, "My friends sometimes call me a sissy because I don't play as long as they do, and because I get good grades. I try to get my mom to let me play more basketball and learn martial arts. I think she is becoming more understanding. She is tough, but what can I say? She runs it, and it's not that bad being valedictorian.

Case Study III

Jamaal Brock is in eighth grade in a private school. He was labeled a behavioral disordered (BD) student in fourth grade at the neighborhood public school. His parents objected at the staff meeting where the decision was made. Mrs. Brock, a schoolteacher, said that if he must be placed, she preferred learning disabled. When children are placed in special education, there is a disproportionate number of Whites placed in LD versus Blacks in BD and EMR. The psychologist, principal, and teacher were adamant that Jamaal should be placed in BD. The Brocks grudgingly conceded, but decided if there was no improvement they would place him in a small private school the following year. The decision in June was not to mainstream Jamaal back into his regular class but to another year of BD. The Brocks, who were unable to place Jamaal in a private school during the middle of the school year at the time of the staff meeting, enrolled their son in a highly acclaimed private school in the fall.

Jamaal is an only child and likes a lot of attention. He has a strong need to be liked by his peers and is easily influenced. He is a good student when he concentrates and pays attention. Howalton is a small private school with a student-teacher ratio of 20 to 1. The school prides itself on being academically challenging, with a good measure of discipline. Students who act up get a chance to visit Mr. Watson and his paddle before they call their parents to explain what happened. I talked to Jamaal about his new school. Jamaal offered these remarks: "At my old school, I had more fun. We would throw spitballs at the girls until we were sent downstairs. That wasn't so bad, because we missed all our assignments. This school doesn't play. I don't know if the school is so strict or the students are chicken, but I do know what went on at PS 192 doesn't go on here. My report card is OK. I got three C's, three B's, and one A. I miss my old friends, but my parents feel this is a better school. I would like to go to a public high school, but I think my parents will send me to another private school. I don't blame them; I haven't been in Mr. Watson's office since fifth grade, and my report card is better."

Case Study IV

Carl Hampton is graduating from high school tonight. Watching proudly from the audience are his mother, his two younger sisters, and his uncle. Tonight may appear easy, but the journey was filled with obstacles. Carl's mother was emotionally and physically abused by her husband, Carl's father. He neglected Carl and his sisters and officially left home when Carl was nine, entering the critical fourth-grade failure syndrome. Coincidentally, his uncle Brian, his mother's younger brother, was just returning home from college after graduation. Uncle Brian stepped in and had a major impact on Carl's life. A few days after graduation, Brian, Carl and I had this conversation. I asked Carl and Brian to describe the graduation journey. Carl said, "I was just out there. My parents were breaking up, my mother said I would be the 'man of the house,' and my friends were into ditching school and stealing. My mother had more than she could handle just paying the bills, and 'raising' my sisters."

Brian commented, and while he spoke, Carl's look of admiration told the story. Uncle Brian had a degree in computer programming and design. Carl did not have his first male teacher until eighth grade. Consequently, if it had not been for his uncle, he would not have seen a Black male academic role model until then. Brian said, "I love my sister, always have, and anything I could do to help, I always tried. I would take Carl to games, programs and sometimes let him just hang out with me on Saturday, but only if he had a good week in school. I would represent him at those programs where fathers' attendance is encouraged. I knew my sister was a good person, but she was weak in choosing men and would possibly be the same in 'raising' one."

Case Study V

Robert Wagner, a seventh-grader, is a small-to-medium-sized kid with curly hair who speaks Standard English. His favorite subjects are math and science, and he has excellent critical thinking skills. He has a knack for taking tests, but doesn't do as well on his report card. He is slightly hyperactive, but teachers have found this occurs when he's not being stimulated. I had an opportunity to talk to Robert's teacher. I asked Mrs. Pierce how Robert was able to avoid the decline in achievement demonstrated by large numbers of Black boys. She stated, "Robert simply has innate ability. A couple of teachers over the years have suggested special placement for Robert, but how can you rationalize that when he often has the highest scores on achievement tests? Robert is not working at his potential, but that does not warrant special education. Most teachers simply like Robert. He's a loving kid, speaks well and avoids getting caught like most boys when doing something mischievous."

In presenting the Conspiracy workshop across the country, frequently someone will offer themselves or someone they know to refute that a conspiracy exists. Often, they expand their premise and suggest that just as they or someone else made it, so can all Black boys. In that same spirit, good-intentioned teachers say, "If I can just save one . . ." Carl Boyd, a good friend of mine, counters with, "If I can just *lose* one." Are we willing to accept the figures that at birth there are 1.03 Black boys to 1.0 Black girls, but at eighteen there are 1.0 Black men to 1.8 Black women? Are we willing to accept the loss of one of every two? What number are you willing to lose? Should we be satisfied that Ron, Lawrence, Jamaal, Carl, and Robert survived the conspiracy? Is there anything we can learn from these case studies that we can use for others less fortunate?

Let's review the factors we have seen in the case studies.

Name	Significant Factors
Ron Gilliam	Athlete, coach
Lawrence Drew	Strong family background, religion, middle-class values, on a continuum from macho (physical) to sissy (mental)
Jamaal Brock	Private school, less negative peer pressure, small student-teacher ratio, higher teacher expectations
Carl Hampton	Significant other apart from parents and coach
Robert Wagner	Innate ability, left-brain thinking (skills ideal for test taking), speaks Standard English, considered physically appealing, and has societal survival skills

Constructive programs can help Black boys enter manhood.

Conversely, those brothers who do not possess these variables are at risk. These brothers can be described as follows:

Not on a school athletic team
Nonacademic household
Lower economic class (cannot afford private school)
Nonreligious
Macho
Influenced by peer group
Low teacher expectations
No significant role model
Right-brain thinking
African features
Black English
No societal survival skills

How many boys do you know who are not on a team, come from a nonacademic household, are impoverished, do not attend church, are aggressive, hang out with a negative peer group, receive low teacher expectations or are placed in special education, are in a large classroom, have no advocate, think better relationally than abstractly, have dark skin with short nappy hair and broad features, speak Black English, and lack Western sophistication? These boys are high risk and are prime candidates for not entering manhood. Every effort, program, person and dollar should be allocated to avoid these tragedies.

In retrospect, please note that these are only partial solutions to our problem. If we know that placing a boy on a school athletic team may encourage him to graduate, it should be pursued. If we can show parents that they do make a difference and that monitoring homework and television and supplementing classwork is significant, it may motivate more parents. If we can show parents that dollars invested in education will bring a greater return than their new car note or clothing accounts, and weekend recreation, it may alter expenditures. If we can show families that "the Lord is able," and to "ask anything that you will in [His] name," it may increase the number of worshipers. If we steer boys to the center of the continuum between macho and sissy, we may be able to redefine manhood.

The chances of boys falling to the right of center (more intellectual than physical) is greatly reduced if parents allow unlimited time on the streets and do not know their son's friends. Not all peer groups are negative; Ron Gilliam's peer group is his teammates, and Lawrence Drew's peer group is his church choir and Simba. Parents need to understand the peer group's desire to evaluate how well a brother can handle himself either athletically or defensively. Parents make a critical mistake going from one extreme to another by moving their sons from the basketball court to piano, rather than half the day in the library or with the piano, and the other half in martial arts or basketball.

If we know the impact that teachers' expectations, student-teacher ratios, and placement in special education have on children's futures, we should visit the classroom at least once, exchange telephone numbers with the teacher, and bring Black professional educators to those special education placement staffings. If we understand that the reason we are "successful" is not because we have some great talent but because someone took the time to help us develop it, we would reach back and help other family, block and church members. Uncle Brian saved a Black boy from futility. If teachers understand that Black children, and particularly Black boys, have a culture that encourages a right-brain approach and alter their curriculum to utilize this strength, and if parents understand that from the fourth grade on, their culture needs to include a left-brain curriculum which encourages analytical applications, we can possibly arrive at an equilibrium.

If teachers could overcome their value judgments of beauty and feel the same way about dark skin, and little Black boys with nappy hair and broad features as they do about Renee, who has light skin, long hair, "pretty" eyes, lace dresses and ribbons in her hair, then Black boys might have an equal chance. If teachers would not place a value judgment on Black English and would learn how to teach Standard English without condemning the child, and if Black parents realized how significant language is to student achievement. We need parents and teachers to talk more to each other and share similar values.

The last reason for that was identified was societal survival skills. Black boys need to be taught, in an African frame of reference, the distinction between a battle and a war. I am reminded of the movie *Ragtime*, starring, Howard Rollins, chose to war rather than battle the White racists who vandelized his new car. He decided that vindicating this act was worth losing his wife, child, job, and ultimately his life. Do you know how many Black boys lose their lives or their freedom because of how they respond to the police? When I was growing up, four of my friends and I were playing ball in an alley. A police car drove down the alley, and two officers asked us if we had seen two teenagers accused of a recent robbery. Four of us answered their questions, but the other decided he "wasn't telling the 'pigs' nothing." The police decided one inconvenience deserved another and took him to the station until his parents signed for his release.

Many Black boys arrive at this position of militancy without having any dialogue with their parents or other respected adults. I began by saying that these societal survival skills need to be taught from an African frame of reference. I am not suggesting that we not stand up for what is right, but I am stating that we need to determine, in a logical manner, how much are we willing to sacrifice. Secondly, standing up for an issue does not negate the importance of *how* you express your views. Thirdly, it concerns me how militant we can be over a car or questions in an alley, but when it's time to vote, boycott, buy Black products and volunteer time to the Black community, we find very few men standing up. There is a difference between a battle and a war. The same people that criticize Dr. King for being passive don't realize that the man believed in nonviolent *resistance* and did not back down on his disdain for the Vietnam War. Dr. King died over Vietnam, not over a brother stepping on his shoes or talking to his lady.

This same failure to differentiate battles and wars follows Black boys into the classroom. Black boys choose to make a war out of situations with their classmates, teachers and principal. In chapter six I made reference to a defiant boy with his arms folded. The boy decided to take a stand. The teacher said, "Get back to work," and he folded his arms and looked either down or away. He chose not to unfold his arms or make eye contact. Before teachers reading this book start nodding their heads, the fundamental lesson here is that Black boys have not been taught other ways to express their manhood. We need men, sensitive female teachers and parents to find healthier expressions.

I believe we have to give our children, especially Black boys, something to lose. Children make foolish choices when they have nothing to lose. Children think twice about drinking, smoking, stealing and becoming pregnant when they have something to lose. Boys shoot people for stepping on their shoes when they don't feel good about themselves. These acts really become suicide missions. When boys behave like this in school, they are indirectly expressing a desire to be expelled because they don't feel good about their achievement. Even the "athlete student" who doesn't like his classes understands the difference between a battle and a war. He will not defy a teacher if he thinks it may impinge upon his privilege to play. A boy who has self-esteem, identified talents, family or racial pride, teacher or coach expectations, scholarship, career plans, or faith in God will make sensible choices between battles and wars.

Large numbers of Black boys have been suspended because they refused to say yes or no ma'am or sir, apologize, take off their hats, alter their walk, talk more softly, smile or change their body language. Robert Wagner survived the conspiracy not because he was quiet in class but because he found that talking more softly protected him from getting caught. When he did get caught he was smart enough to smile at the teacher, apologize and get back to work. He did not think talking to his friend in class was a war. It was a battle he would like to have won, but if he fought the battle and lost, he would not be around for the war. We have lost a lot of brothers in battle; *and in the war to save the Black family, we have very few brothers available.*

You cannot teach a child you do not love. You cannot teach a child you do not respect. You cannot teach a child you do not understand.

   The objective of this book has been to pinpoint why, when and how African American boys are denied the skills necessary for manhood, and what strategies can be developed to negate the conspiracy and enhance African American male development. We are involved in a cultural struggle. Culture is more than your music, dress or the food you eat. Culture is everything you do; it's your lifestyle which results from the way you perceive yourself within the context of the world. A part of our culture should be the successful transition from boyhood to manhood. One measure of cultural success can be defined as securing a high ratio of boys making this transition. We must develop cultural strategies, changes in our lifestyle, which achieve this objective.

   I sincerely believe it takes a man to develop boys into men. Please do not misquote or misinterpret me; I did not say a single female parent could not develop her son into a man, but she does not need to attempt such a significant act alone. African American social scientists were quick to refute Moynihan's position that African American families lacked male input by illustrating our extended family tradition. Sixty-two percent of our children are reared by single parents, but very few families received no input from a male figure, e.g., grandfather, father, brother, uncle, nephew, cousin, neighbor, lover or friend. While social scientists were theoretically correct to negate Moynihan's analysis, until we consciously utilize our extended family tradition to eradicate the conspiracy, to whose benefit is its existence? Very few African American women are consciously aware that their son needs a positive role model, that the family, streets, television, school and church institutions come up lacking, and that a concerted effort between them and a male extended family member must actively fill the void. Until African American women admit that only men can make boys into men, and African American men become responsible for giving direction to at least one male child, the conspiracy will continue.

   Every concerned African American man should ask himself if he is providing some positive direction to at least one male child. Concerned administrators, teachers and parents should solicit men to speak in the schools that sorely lack a male presence. I don't mean asking celebrities such as Andrew Young and Jesse Jackson, but your local bus driver, mailman, etc., who in his own way is trying to be consistent. Hopefully, this will not only inspire male children but motivate African American men to become more responsible. African American men, especially teachers, should offer to teach at least one year in the primary division. Librarians and teachers should make available as much literature as possible about African American male achievements, particularly outside the professions of entertainment and sports.

Parents are quick to say, "Television is destroying the minds of our children, and I can't keep up with the boy when he goes outside." My response is: as powerful as ABC, CBS, NBC, Fox and CABLE are, they cannot force you to turn your television set on. If television is a problem, it is because you are not controlling your household. If the streets are a problem, it is because you are not controlling your child's schedule. Children cannot raise themselves, and parents should not allow television or the streets to try. Conscientious parents create activities to replace television viewing.

A single parent is different from single parenting. Single parenting assumes the entire burden; conscientious single parents enroll their child in martial arts, little league, carpentry, band, etc. Concerned parents realize their children want to interact with their peer group, but *what* they do should receive your input. My extended family, grandparents, aunts, uncles, neighbors and friends exposed me very early to the dangers of the streets with functional field trips to drug abuse centers, jails, and neighborhood hospitals on Friday evenings. The experiences are memorable to this day and have enhanced my desire to have a life-style free of dope and crime.

The business community could benefit from a reduction of street crime. Black businesses are saddled with higher costs because of vandalism, inventory shrinkage, and having to employ additional security. Sales decline because the streets are not safe for customers.

Businesses could help their plight by employing a teenager, if for nothing more than 5 to 10 hours per week. This short term expense may pay handsome long-term benefits with less inventory shrinkage, reduction of armed guards, and increased sales due to safe streets. Businesses should take full advantage of publicity to inform the African American community of their intentions. Black businesses should remove the "attitude" that they are doing the customer a "favor" with their existence, and express their concern for their customers. (Some European Americans may be racist, but most show their satisfaction with your patronage.) I am also a strong advocate of youth volunteering their services to learn necessary skills. One summer, I chose to volunteer with an electrical firm. The employer could not believe I wanted to volunteer, and I imagine his shock motivated his approval. During my internship I began to receive bus money, and a small salary, but more importantly, I learned the mechanics of electricity that will last a lifetime!

The million-dollar question that every group, conference, and concerned committee asks is, "How are we going to reach men between 18 and 30?" It often amazes me that people who raise this question discuss it in the Hyatt Regency, the Marriott and the Hilton, while the people they're discussing have very little opportunity to pay the registration fees or to be comfortable sharing in this kind of setting. I often wonder whether they really want to reach this group. It appears to me that most people are comfortable talking with people that have similar experiences. Some vegetarians don't feel comfortable around people that eat chitterlings. Some Christians are not comfortable being around Muslims and vice-versa. Some people that live in the suburbs and are middle income aren't comfortable around people who live in the city and may be lower income. Do we honestly think that having a conference about the plight of Black males at a downtown hotel can solve their problems? Do we leave these conferences with a plan of action that will take us to their community? Do we really love the very brothers that we talk about?

I will never forget a National Urban League Conference held in Atlanta. A street brother found out about the program and came over to the hotel and asked whether he could earn his registration fee by doing some work because he wanted to participate. It just blew the minds of most of the participants that were there.

In order to save older men 18 to 25-years-old, we are going to have to devise a marketing outreach strategy. A design that was similar to that of Marcus Garvey, the Nation of Islam, Jehovah's Witnesses and progressive Christian churches practicing liberation theology. We will not save this group with institutions that believe the only answers exist *inside* of their buildings. I am so glad that Elijah Muhammad did not wait for Detroit Red to be released from prison to find him.

The review of teenage pregnancy programs nationwide indicates that 90 percent counsel the female. We must believe that men are also responsible. Maybe we feel that this group is too difficult to work with, or that it's too burdensome to organize them. I reiterate: I think the first step in solving the problem for this age group is to ask ourselves, "Do we really want to interact with this group directly?" If the answer is yes, then the second step is to quit having conferences at downtown hotels and have the programs in the community where these brothers reside.

Also, we have to quit designing these teenage pregnancy programs around the table with coffee and doughnuts. I suggest that a better way to attract males would be with male counselors. A man would play basketball with the male clients and discuss the same issues without coffee and doughnuts. For the basketball court, a counselor could substitute a weight room, a vocational training room or a pooltable, all situations that many female social workers wouldn't even consider.

As much as I dislike Jehovah's Witnesses knocking on my door, I respect them for believing in their position and being willing to take it to the streets. This is what we are going to have to do if we're going to save our males in the prime of their lives.

After we have resolved the major hurdle, the will and the commitment to want to interact with the men directly, we must then provide them with shock treatment.

This shock treatment would include taking them to a prison and letting them talk to hard core but now conscious inmates. We would take them to a drug abuse program and let them witness how difficult it is to withdraw. It would include a trip to a public hospital on a Saturday at midnight to view the tremendous volume of emergencies, and then to the morgue. It would incorporate a movie on what crack does to the brain.

I am not naive. I am very much aware that for some brothers these experiences will not be a shock treatment but will be business as usual. This is why my research has tried to concentrate on intervening at earlier ages. It is more difficult to shock someone who has experienced 18 or more years of a negative lifestyle. For many of our brothers who are moving as fast as Detroit Red, only prison provides the opportunity to fully know their predicament. We have a very "captive audience" of approximately 1,500,000 African American males waiting for dedicated teachers who can provide shock treatment.

The African American community cannot afford to lose this many men, while America builds a billion-dollar prison industry with poor White workers in rural America — business that only rehabilitates 15 percent and has an 85 percent recidivism rate. We need a major organization to negotiate with wardens and have conferences at prison sites. Minister Farrakhan from the Nation of Islam has already said that he wants prisoners released and taken to an independent land site. What are other leaders saying?

Returning to my original statement that these activities are forms of shock treatment, unfortunately, for some of our males in this age group, this will not be shocking. Some have experienced greater atrocities and more horrifying experiences. However, there are some males who would be affected by this approach and for that reason it needs to be implemented. For those that would not be, we will unfortunately see them in prisons and hopefully not the morgue. As long as they are *alive*, we have an opportunity to *rehabilitate*.

The second step after the shock treatment I label, Kunjufu's Holistic Approach, which includes spirituality, African and African American history, an understanding of racism, time management, talent identification and development, proper dict and nutrition, an understanding of economics, becoming a member of a positive peer group, and joining an organization. Let's review these areas in some detail.

I believe that any one of these areas can develop our males to reach their full potential. The more factors working congruently, the more effective the process. When I provide consultations to social service agencies, I recommend that the staff determine which members will be responsible for each area. Any client participating in the program will have to interact with each staff member. The staff will expose the participant to the necessary information in all areas.

Spirituality

One of the major reasons for the rehabilitation of Malcolm X was his coming to grips with his relationship with God. I am a Christian and I am very proud of my relationship with my Lord and Savior, Jesus Christ. This book is not being used as a vehicle to argue about God but to encourage males to submit themselves to God. I have read numerous articles on this topic; submission in any form is difficult for males. I believe that this is also the major reason for males having a much higher suicide rate than females — the lack of desire to submit and share their problems with God. In this area, males should be taught the necessity of submission and then should learn how to pray and read Scriptures.

African and African American History

I'm positive that one of the major reasons for the success of the Nation of Islam and most Christian churches that have been able to attract men is they have provided the group with an opportunity to learn and appreciate their culture. Many men have been taught very little about their history. They, like our people, have been given a history in which on the first day we were in Africa, the second day we were on the boat, and the remaining part of the course was slavery in America. I suggest that if African American men were able to internalize the personalities of Imhotep, King Ramses, King Akhenaten, Toussaint-Louverture, Nat Turner, Marcus Garvey, Dr. King and Malcolm X, we would experience self-love. Self-hatred and homicide would decline.

Racism

Many of our males have not been taught that racism is a sign of insecurity, not inferiority. People that are secure are comfortable with differences. Only insecure people have to rationalize that because they are different. If African people were inferior, then there would be no need for discrimination. I argue that racists know more about African Americans than we know about ourselves. In this section, we would explain to the men how special they are and how afraid this country is of African American males reaching their full potential. This explains lynching and castration.

Time Management

Time is the most important resource. It is more valuable than cars, clothes, money or a mansion. Yet many African American males waste the most valuable resource standing on the corner. They have allowed this country to reduce them to a dollar bill. If the country no longer employs them, they hang out on the corner and sulk. We would establish the need for African American men to develop a time chart, so that they will become conscious of how they're spending their twenty-four hours. We will also encourage them so that when they cannot find work, they will use their time either to acquire a skill or to volunteer in an area where they can learn.

Talent Identification and Development

In my earlier book, *Motivating and Preparing Black Youth For Success*, I indicated that many people will never find their talents. It is important that a counselor or a concerned adult encourages males to find out what their interests and strengths are and to match careers with their interests. I want to stress that talents are not just in sports and music, but are also in reading, writing, language arts, computer skills, concentration skills, eye-hand coordination, and visual, creative, and mechanical skills.

Diet and Nutrition

African American males probably have the worst diet in America. They smoke more cigarettes, drink more liquor, use more hard drugs, eat less fruit and salad, and consume more fried foods and red meat than any other group. We need to teach African American men how to reduce their red meat intake, to consume more natural products, to drink more water, exercise, and stay away from nicotine, caffeine and hard drugs. When Malcolm was released from prison, rumor has it that he was so disciplined that he never chewed gum or ate candy any more.

Economics

Economics is a very important area, especially for the 18-25 age group. History and culture alone are not going to be effective if we cannot provide men employment. One of the major reasons for the success of the Nation of Islam, besides introducing the males to God, is giving them 300 newspapers, fish, bean pies and power products to sell. As much as I dislike the drug dealer, he can be credited with providing jobs in our community, while the Black middle class works for someone else. We need African Americans that will create jobs in our neighborhoods. We are not going to save this age group without providing them with employment. There are only two ways of doing it: *asking* the government to provide a national job bill and/or *providing* the jobs in our community ourselves by spending $300 billion with each other.

Peer Group and Organizations

When you allow anyone to have bad habits for 18-25 years, it is very difficult to break those bad habits. I often tell youth that the most important decision of their lives will be the friends they choose. I say that the group that you *spend* time with will be the group that you *end* up with and it will shape your personality. Therefore, a very easy way to become successful is to choose positive friends and organizations. Unfortunately, the gangs don't receive an enormous amount of competition from other groups in the community. The combination of their material possessions and the lack of competition has allowed the gangs to become successful.

I'd like to offer this theoretical paradigm that addresses the conspiracy to destroy Black boys.

1. What is the problem?
2. What caused the problem?
3. What are the solutions?
4. How can they be implemented?

In a typical one-hour workshop, you receive fifty-five minutes for the problem, four minutes for causes, one minute for solutions and no time for implementation.

The Problem

By the year 2020, 70 percent of all Black males will be unavailable to Black women. Eighty-five percent of the African American children that are placed in special education are African American males. Approximately 1.5 million African American males are in penal institutions. Forty-seven percent of the penal population is African American. Only 3.5 percent of college students are African American. We receive 37 percent of all school suspensions. We have the lowest life expectancy. We have the highest homicide and cancer rates. Thirty-one percent of African American males ages 18-25 are unemployed. (This is a very conservative figure; some people think that it's closer to 40 to 45 percent.)

The Causes

White male supremacy/institutional racism
A capital intensive economy
Drugs
The male socialization process
Double child rearing standards among parents
Parental apathy
Low teacher expectations
Lack of understanding of the male learning styles
Negative peer pressure and gangs
The lack of positive male role models

Solutions

In order to correct the problems, the solutions have to address the causes.

Racism. We must understand and resist racism and empower our community to reach its full potential.

High tech economy. We must lobby for a high tech economy which would include a federal job bill, a reduction in the defense budget, more money allocated for education and training, a reduction in foreign imports, and Black economic development.

Drugs. We must patrol our borders, enhance self-esteem, prevent stores from selling drug paraphernalia, use the money from drug busts for community programs, allocate more money for treatment and increase community watch groups.

Male socialization process. We must increase Rites of Passage programs and produce programs for electronic media to portray Black male's strengths, mental and spiritual.

Parental double standard. We must have workshops and books for parents that inform them of the necessity to teach their sons and daughters to be equally responsible and self-sufficient.

Parental apathy. We must market the PTA to attract parents, increase the number of families receiving services from Chapter One and Head Start, and provide more workshops.

Lower teacher expectations. We must have mandatory in-service training on expectations from Africentric educational scholars.

Learning styles. We must have mandatory in-service training using books that explain the race sensitive differences of boys, girls maturation rates and learning styles. A moratorium on special education placement for Black boys, a Black male classroom and attracting more Black male teachers to the classroom.

Negative peer pressure and gangs. We must have programs that teach boys the distinction between battles and wars, conflict management and peer group monitoring.

Lack of male role models. We must have a media campaign showing Cub Scouts, classroom teachers and other role models all being female and its dire consequences for Black male development.

How can we develop an environment where Cody could have remained Cody (See Chapter 11) or become Sanyika? How can we reconcile Marlon's (See Chapter 8) Monday morning reality? How can we increase the probability beyond two percent that Jerome (See Chapter 10) graduates from college and either becomes an entrepreneur or is gainfully employed in the area in which he studied? How can we assist mothers raising sons alone?

Over the past two decades, the problems of African American males have escalated, and people often ask me, do you believe you're making a difference? Do you believe it is possible to save the African American male? My favorite answer is always one of optimism. I still believe that we have more on our side than they have on theirs, that all things are possible for those that love the Lord. Presently, we are experiencing a Friday afternoon, but there will be a Sunday morning rising. If we give up, we automatically lose. Only if we dare to struggle do we dare to win. The quantitative answer is listed below. Over the past two decades we have developed:

1) Over 200 Rites of Passage programs nationwide
2) 1,000 mentoring and role model programs
3) Over 100 Black male classrooms
4) Over 10 Black male schools
5) Hundreds of workshops to analyze the issues
6) Over 30 books written on the subject
7) Over 20 colleges that offer scholarships for African American males that want to major in education
8) Five states with commissions to address the problems of the African American male
9) Lessons on teenage sexuality and responsibility provided by Project Alpha and the Urban League

I believe after 30 books and hundreds of workshops and conferences, we know the problems, what caused them and the solutions. The major question is, what prevents us from moving from theory to practice? Why have we not implemented our solutions? The reasons and areas of implementation are listed below:

1) Lack of information
2) Time
3) Work
4) Money
5) Bootstrap Theory
6) Ego
7) Fear
8) Personal problems
9) No consequences
10) Lack of faith
11) Lack of trust
12) Resistance to change

Lack of information

There remains a wide disparity between what the conscious members know and the masses. If the masses don't read and will not pay $10-$100 for workshops and conferences, and are completely dependent on the mass media for information, how will they be informed?

Time

Many people work eight hours per day, commute two hours, eat three meals and sleep eight eight hours. This schedule allows only three hours left in a day. If they choose to spend that time watching television, talking on the telephone, listening to music, playing golf, bowling, working out in the health club and on other recreational and entertainment activities, there may not be time to stop the conspiracy. I suggest everyone chart their twenty-four hours and strive toward giving more hours back to the community.

Work

I noticed that when we started Community of Men and had two months to strategize, we had a building full of talkers. I noticed that in my pastor's manhood class, where all they had to do was listen, the numbers were staggering. But when it was time to work in Rites of Passage, Role Model, Mentoring, crime watch groups, junior business leagues, etc., the numbers plummeted. It is obvious that talk is cheap and work is divine. When people want to talk with me now, I tell them to put it in writing. I tell them to meet me at the Rites of Passage program or at Community of Men. We can talk while we work. I don't mind talking as long as we are working.

Money

In order to save our children, we will have to put money on the table. We may have to provide the capital to start the businesses. We may have to buy the T-shirts and provide the money for the bus trips. We may have to finance our youth's business plans. Two of our largest organizations, the NAACP and the Urban League, are both dependent upon outside resources to finance their programs. We can't finance our liberation struggle on grants.

Bootstrap Theory

This theory is led by people like Clarence Thomas, Thomas Sowell, and Shelby Steele and others who believe they made it because of hard work and the Bootstrap Theory. They believe all problems can be solved with individual effort. The unfortunate thing is that they attribute self-help to the Republican party and not African people. Secondly, they really do believe that they made it completely off the Bootstrap Theory and that the role model that inspired them in sixth grade and the mentor that inspired them to attend college had nothing to do with their lives. I would like to ask the bookstrap advocates if they would be successful if they were the offspring of a fourteen-year-old mother on crack who never told them she loved them, and there was no significant role model in their lives. Would they still be successful?

Ego

Many African American men have an ego problem working with other men. Many men are more effective when they work individually with boys in Little League baseball or Boy Scouts rather than working in organizations such as Rites of Passage, Role Model or crime watch groups, where there are numerous men involved in the activities.

In our organizations we have been effective by using the motto: Leaving the ego at the door. We try to develop all men to be leaders in the organization. One of the ways I evaluate an organization, especially the leader or president, is the level of responsibility given to the "Lieutenants." It is very disappointing to see men involved in Rites of Passage argue in front of the boys on who's blacker than who, who speaks more fluent Swahili, who has read the most Black books, who has been to Africa the most times and who's been involved in the liberation struggle the longest.

Fear

The more successful we become at developing Black boys into men the more we become a threat to White male supremacy. By doing so, many of us are afraid we are going to lose our jobs, contracts, houses and cars. We begin to compromise. It has been said that if you give an African American man a good job, you can write him off from the liberation struggle. The job becomes more important than freedom. My high school history teacher describes this as our materialism being incompatible with our quest for freedom.

Personal problems

Many African Americans are not involved in the liberation struggle because they have personal problems that have to be resolved. A person cannot be faulted if he has an invalid relative at home that he needs to take care of, if there is someone hospitalized, if there is a wayward cousin or family member that has some deep-seated emotional problems that need to be addressed. Can you criticize a brother who can't make the meeting because he has several young children? What if the brother has high blood pressure or prostate cancer?

No consequences

Teachers are still paid regardless of whether children learn to read. We had 175 men involved in our crime watch group and now we have 21. There were no consequences for the men choosing to do something else or doing nothing. The African American community knows a brother impregnated a sister but will not hold him accountable for his behavior. Without consequences, the liberation struggle is reduced to people's whims.

Lack of faith

Deep down in our gut, do we believe? Do we have the faith? Do we have the willpower to believe that we can develop Black boys into men? Have our spirits been so broken that we believe the only boys that we can save are between the ages of five and nine? Do we have enough faith to believe that we can save boys aged nine to thirteen or thirteen to eighteen? The problem with faith is that you can't buy it or discover it intellectually. You either have it or you don't; you either believe or you don't. Scripture teaches, "Faith is the substance of things hoped for, the evidence of things unseen." You don't believe with you ears; you don't smell with your eyes; you don't see with your heart. The only way to believe is to believe with your heart. We have to believe that we can win.

Lack of trust

If all of us gave one dollar and there are 40 million of us we would have 40 million dollars. If our 150 largest organizations chose not to meet in White hotels for one year, we would save 16 billion dollars. The problem is, who would we trust to hold that kind of money?

Resistance to change

Many Black churches, colleges and civil rights organizations' favorite slogan is, "It should be obvious that this way is not working." We must identify new ways to save our boys. Why are boys more committed to the gangs and frats than to the Lord and the liberation struggle? What can we learn from gangs to reclaim our boys?

In closing, to reclaim our boys will require marathon runners. The race against White supremacy can't be done with sprinters. I am often asked, how long will it take? Slavery in America lasted 246 years or 22 generations. We have been physically free for 130 years or six to seven generations. Some people feel it will take another 15 generations before African people return to the zenith we created in Kemet. I can't speculate on 15 generations, but on my day of judgment, I want God to say, "Well done, good and faithful servant."

References

Chapter 1

1. Flint, John. Cecil Rhodes. Little Brown, Boston, MA, 1974, pp. 248-252.

2. Browder, Anthony. *Nile Valley Contributions to Civilization*. Institute of Karmic Guidance, Washington, D.C., 1992, pp. 17-18.

3. Sklar, Holly. *Trilateralism*. South End Press, Boston, MA, 1981, p. 1.

4. Wilhelm, Sidney. *Who Needs the Negro?* Doubleday, New York, N.Y., 1970, p. xiii.

5. Epperson, A. Ralph. *The New World Order*. Publius Press, 1990, p. xiii.

6. Welsing, Frances Cress. *The Isis Papers*. Third World Press, Chicago, IL, 1991, pp. x, xi.

Chapter 2

1. U.S. Statistical Abstract 2003

2. Wilson, Amos. *Developmental Psychology of the Black Child*, (New York: Africana Research Publications, 1978), p. 46.

3. McGuinness, Diane. *When Children Don't Learn*, (New York: Basic Books), p. 47.

4. Ibid., p. 21.

5. Ibid., pp. 77-78.

6. Kunjufu, Jawanza. *Developing Positive Self-Images and Discipline in Black Children*, (Chicago: African American Images, 1984), pp. 38-39.

7. McGuinness, op cit., pp. 190-192.

8. Ray Rist, "Student Social Class and Teacher Expectations," *Harvard Educational Review*, Volume 40, No. 3, August, 1970, pp. 411-449.

9. Kunjufu, op. cit., p. 17.

Chapter 3

1. Harry Morgan, "How Schools Fail Black Children," *Social Policy*, Jan.-Feb., 1980, pp. 49-54.

2. An unpublished survey made by the author.

3. Nancy Arnez, "Implementation of Desegregation as a Discriminating Process," *Journal of Negro Foundation*, 1978, pp. 28-45.

4. Hare, Bruce. *Black Girls: A Comparative Analysis of Self-Perception and Achievement by Race, Sex and Socio-Economic Background*, (Baltimore: Center For Social Organization of Schools, John Hopkins University, 1979).

5. James Patton, "The Black Male's Struggle For An Education," ed. Gary Lawrence (Beverly Hills: Black Men Sage, 1981), p. 205.

6. U.S. Statistical Abstract 2003

7. Perkins, Eugene. *Home is a Dirty Street*, (Chicago: Third World Press, 1975), pp. 17, 26.

Chapter 6

1. Excerpts from "The Challenge of Blackness" delivered by Lerone Bennett at the Institute of Black World in Atlanta, GA, 1972.

Chapter 7

1. Ronald Edmonds, "Effective Schools for the Urban Poor." *Educational Leadership*, October, 1979, pp. 16-22.

2. Excerpts from "Black Children, Their Roots, Culture, and Learning Styles," delivered by Janice Hale in Kenosha, Wisconsin, 1986.

3. Hale, Janice. *Black Children, Their Roots, Culture, and Learning Styles*. (Provo: Brigham Young University Press, 1982), pp. 32-35.

4. *Culture Linguistic Approach Social Studies Manual*, Chicago: Northeastern Illinois University Center for Inner City Studies, 1974, pp. 14-15.

Chapter 8

1. Wilson, Amos. *Black on Black Violence* (New York: African World Info Systems, 1990), pp. 168-169.

Chapter 9

1. Margo Crawford, "Black Teachers Call Halt to Seasoning," (*Black Books Bulletin*, Vol. 2 No. 4, Chicago, Institute of Positive Education, 1974), p. 45.

2. Goldberg, Herb. *Hazards of Being Male*, (New York: Signet, 1976), pp. 43-44.

3. Brown, Michael. *Image of a Man*, (New York: East Publications, 1976), p. 6.

4. McDavid, John and Garwood. *Understanding Children*, (Washington, D.C.: Health, Lexington, 1978), p. 361.

5. "The Difference in the Sexes," *Newsweek*, May 18, 1981, pp. 74-75.

6. McDavid, op. cit. p. 348.

7. Wilson, Amos. *Developmental Psychology of the Black Child*, (New York: Africana Research Publications, 1978), pp. 94-96.

8. United Nations Yearbook, 2003

9. Goldberg, op. cit. pp. 172 and 176.

10. Liebow, Elliot. *Tally's Corner*, (Boston: Little, Brown, 1967), pp. 210-213.

11. Gary, Lawrence. *Black Men*, (Beverly Hills: Sage, 1981), p. 53.

12. United States Statistical Abstract, 2003

13. Raphael, Ray. *The Men From Boys*, (Lincoln: University of Nebraska Press, 1988), p. xi.

14. Fair, Frank. *Orita For Black Youth*, (Valley Forge: Judson Press, 1977), p. 11.

15. Hare, Nathan and Julia. *Bringing The Black Boy to Manhood*. (San Francisco: Black Think Tank, 1985), p. 20.

16. Hare, p. 28.

17. Ibid., p. 26.

Chapter 10

1. Fleming, Jacqueline. *Blacks in College*, (San Francisco: Jossey-Bass, 1984), pp. 141-145.

Chapter 11

1. Bing, Leon. *Do or Die*, (New York: Harper Collins, 1991), p. 237.

2. Scott, Cody. *Monster: The Autobiography of an L.A. Gang Member*, 1993, p. 278.

3. Wilson, op. cit., pp. X, 83.

4. Ibid., p. 129.

5. Ibid., p. 123.

PLEDGE ON BLACK MANHOOD

I am the Black man
Some know me as Imhotep, Ramses,
Martin or Malcolm.
Others know me as the brother on the corner
or in jail.

I am both, Detroit Red and Malcolm.
From this day forward, I pledge my life
to the liberation of my people.
I will put God first in my life.
Black women will feel safe when they see me.
I will be a supportive, responsible,
and loving husband.
I will hug, talk and listen to, and
educate my children.
I will be involved in the Scouts,
Role Model and Rites-of-Passage.

Why?
Because I am the Black man - the original man,
the one and only.
The one that other men are afraid of,
because they know whenever
I've seized the opportunity - I succeed.

JAWANZA KUNJUFU

Why Some Black Boys Don't Believe They Need Men in Their Lives

❖ It is difficult to admit that you need someone whom you have never (or seldom) experienced.

❖ They have never experienced a man in authority.

❖ Their mother told them that they were the *man of the house*.

❖ If they are the man of the house, they do not need, nor value a male teacher, counselor, dean, administrator, coach, mentor, or any other male in authority.

❖ They do not need a man to provide, because their mother is the provider.

❖ They do not need a man to teach them how to farm or work in a factory, because those jobs are obsolete.

❖ They do not need a man to teach them how to develop skills in the area of information systems, because either a woman can do that, or they do not value those skills.

❖ They do not need a man to teach them about sexuality, because they "think" that *life* has adequately educated them.

❖ They do not need a man to teach them how to rap, play basketball, or fight, because their friends can teach them.

❖ They do not need a man to teach them how to drive, because schools provide drivers education classes.

❖ They do not need a man to teach them how to repair things, because America has decided that it's cheaper to just discard the old and purchase the new (all from overseas.)

❖ They do not need a man to teach them how to treat a lady because certain media, as well as their peers have them believing that the female doesn't desire nor deserve to be treated with respect.

❖ They do not need a man to teach them how to be a father because they "unknowingly" have decided to be a sperm donor.

❖ Finally, because their mother appointed them the *man of the house*, they may never have a need to leave!

Notes